80 YEARS
AEC

Alan Townsin
and
Brian Goulding

Senior Publications : Glossop : Derbyshire : England

© August 1992

ISBN 0 86317 177 X

OTHER AEC BOOKS AND COMPANION VOLUMES

Best of British Buses

AEC Regals
AEC Regents 1929-42
The AEC Q family
Post-War Regents

Leyland Titans 1927-42
Leyland Tigers 1927-81
The Utilities
Post-War Titans
Post-War Daimlers

Operators

Aldershot & District
Brighton Hove & District
Crosville
Cumberland
Dodds/AA Motor Services
Liverpool Buses
LUT/SLT
Liverpool Buses
Northampton
Ribble
Southdown
Thames Valley
Glasgow Buses
Forty Years with London Transport
London Bus Diary
South Wales Transport
Shearings
SHMD

British Bus Story

1946-50 A Golden Age
1950s A Wind of Change
1960s Turbulent Times
Early 'Seventies
Late 'Seventies
Early 'Eighties

Bodybuilders

Alexander Coachbuilders
Northern Counties of Wigan
Park Royal (2 Vols)
Roe Coachbuilders
Eastern Coach Works

List of all titles available on receipt of SAE

Produced electronically for the Publishers by
Mopok Graphics, 128 Pikes Lane, Glossop, Derbyshire
Printed and bound in Great Britain

Contents

Introduction   4
A brief history of AEC and its products   5
Southall scenes   21
Walthamstow warriors   25
6-type survivors   27
Military interlude   33
Mark III – a golden age   37
Mediumweights   41
AEC world-wide   47
1 – Portugal   47
2 – Malta   51
3 – Greece   52
4 – Cyprus   53
5 – Iraq   55
6 – Iran   55
8 – Hong Kong   56
7 – Malaya   56
9 – Uganda   57
10 – Zimbabwe   57
11 – South Africa   58
12 – Australia   61
13 – New Zealand   68
14 – Uruguay   71
15 – Argentina   76
16 – Peru   77
17 – West Indies   78
18 – Canada   79
Acknowledgements   80

AEC or AEC-related vehicles are still to be found in several countries not included in the contents list above. In France, for example, the Willeme concern of Nanterre offered AEC engines in its goods models from 1962 to about 1970, beginning with the AV470 and AV690 and progressing in later years to the AV691 and AV760. In general, only engines were supplied, but the K301 model had an AV470 unit and an AEC rear axle as well as an AEC grille applied to the Willeme cab – this 1965 example is preserved by F. Michel of St. Remy, who supplied the photograph. Another type, the K303 was in effect a complete AEC with the Ergomatic cab. In Belgium, once quite an active market for AEC, it is thought that only one is remaining, a 1960 Mandator tractive unit originally owned by Belgian BP and now preserved by Fernend Van de Plas.

Introduction

The 80th anniversary of the formation of AEC in June 1912 is an appropriate time to consider what the concern achieved during the period of just under 67 years as a vehicle manufacturer and how strong a legacy remains. The emphasis in this volume is on the AEC vehicles which still exist. Just how many there are is quite impossible to say, for they are distributed almost all over the world, many of them still earning their keep in locations almost as varied as they are numerous, quite apart from the growing numbers of preserved vehicles.

When it is remembered that the last examples to be built are at least thirteen years old in terms of the date the chassis were assembled – and a considerably older minimum age for many models of which production ended long before the factory closed – the extent to which AEC vehicles are to be seen in everyday use is remarkable. It is often the case with vehicles of any make that factory support in terms of spares availability is withdrawn, even for the products of firms still in business, after ten years beyond the date the model was taken out of production. Yet there are 40-year-old RT-type double-deckers still on sightseeing duty in California, for example, and it would not be difficult to find a Matador on logging or recovery duties with about half a century of service behind it, in many parts of Britain and elsewhere. Here and there, even older examples can be found still in regular use, and by no means confined to places with cultural or economic ties to Britain, even though AEC was strong in almost all parts of the British Empire. Mere youngsters of 20-30 year ages are almost commonplace.

A haulier or bus operator in Uruguay still running Mark III goods or passengers models, just like a preservationist with a similar model in Britain, has long since learnt to live without expecting to be able to obtain spares via an official factory network. This is perhaps as eloquent a testimony as any of the durability of AEC vehicles – though items do eventually wear out, the basic reliability is good enough for operators to persevere and find ways round any problems. In some ways, the more remote the location the greater the self-reliance developed.

On the other hand, it is certainly true that AEC, both as a company and in its products, was blessed with what can only be described as charisma throughout much of its life.

Imaginative management with an interest in artistic merit was a characteristic which ran right through the Underground group of companies, fostered by Lord Ashfield himself, and hence fed into AEC from the start – the bullseye emblem still familiar on London tube stations was used as a basis for the AEC monogram from quite early on.

However, it was the arrival of G. J. Rackham as Chief Engineer in 1928 which really brought artistic flair. He was one of the happy breed of 'aesthetic' engineers who combined function and form. His chassis always had well-balanced proportions and although AEC did not build bodywork, he did his best to ensure that this applied to completed vehicles, while such individual items as the traditional-style AEC radiator of 1929 onwards and the Mark III goods cab were models of subtlety which remain satisfying to the eye even when seen repeatedly.

So just as, say, Sir Nigel Gresley's 'Flying Scotsman' locomotive, R. J. Mitchell's Spitfire fighter aircraft and Ettore Bugatti's cars remain models of visual as well as purposeful design, the same can be said of many AEC vehicles, often accounting for much of the devotion of those who preserve them.

But the charisma went wider than the vehicles, for the firm was adept at publicity, with its lively house journal, *AEC Gazette* which was more than a mere propaganda weapon, for there was no lack of interesting ventures to report, making copies still much prized.

This volume quite deliberately puts most of the emphasis on the survivors, working or honourably retired, whether showing the effects of hard use over many years, dusty and rusty as discovered years after being discarded, or immaculate. As will be evident, they include early and late models, passenger and goods, civilian and military, giving a remarkable indication of the variety of uses to which products of the Southall – and, earlier, Walthamstow – factory have been put and the huge list of users and locations in which they were to be found.

Since the corresponding volume marking the 75th anniversary, the AEC Society has gone from strength to strength and the number of vehicles rescued for preservation steadily grows. The old firm may have gone but it and its products are in no danger of being forgotten.

Alan Townsin
Steventon, 1992

A brief history of AEC and its products

There were key events in the AEC story which influenced the design of the vehicles built at various periods and played a major part in their character, so it is helpful to include an outline of the story.

Although the Associated Equipment Co Ltd – an un-imaginative-seeming name for what was to become so famous a concern – was formed 80 years ago, on 12th June 1912, we have to go back much further to trace its roots.

The use of motor buses in London began just about the turn of the century, at first on a very small scale – by contrast horse buses were on the streets in huge numbers. Among the users of the new form of vehicle was the freshly set-up London Motor Omnibus Co Ltd, from 1905 using the fleetname Vanguard, and it proved to be among the more successful of the pioneers. At first, like most of the early ventures, it used imported vehicles, but decided to set about building its own, establishing a factory for the purpose at Walthamstow on the eastern

outskirts of London. A subsidiary, Motor Omnibus Construction Ltd, was set up for the purpose and small numbers of MOC vehicles were built in 1906-7.

In 1908 a merger of Vanguard with two other leading motor bus operators in London produced a combined fleet of 994 vehicles. One of these was the London General Omnibus Co Ltd, which had been founded in 1855 to amalgamate horse bus businesses – its maximum fleet of these was 1,416, reached in 1905. It was the largest concern in the 1908 merger so the Vanguard name disappeared, although the telegraphic address 'Vangastow' was retained and continued to be used by AEC to the end.

By then, the LGOC was firmly committed to replacement of its horse buses and decided to develop the Walthamstow factory to build most of the motor bus chassis it needed, basing fresh designs on experience of the various makes in the existing combined fleet. After the initial X-

type, the B-type was developed in 1910. Although basically simple and conventional, apart from its silent-chain gearbox (designed to overcome the then common problem of excessive gear noise) it set new standards of reliability and quiet running. As was standard practice at the time, it was of so-called 'normal-control' (bonneted) layout, the open-top double-deck body seating 34 passengers.

At least as important, the Walthamstow factory was developed to allow volume production at about 1,000 per year, a level virtually unknown in Britain at that time. At the beginning of 1912, the LGOC was taken over by the Underground group, with Albert Stanley, later Lord Ashfield, as its Managing Director, and thus became part of the organisation already responsible for the tube and other electric railways in London.

The decision to set up the Associated Equipment Co Ltd in June of that year to run the Walthamstow

The Walthamstow factory was already busily producing B-type chassis when AEC was set up as a separate concern in 1912 to take over that aspect of the London General Omnibus Co's activities. Quite a number of B-type buses saw further service outside London, most famously those that were sent to France as troop-carriers in the 1914-18 war. More peaceful is this scene in Great Yarmouth in the 'twenties, where the Corporation purchased three ex-LGOC examples in 1920, replacing them with three more in 1925. Great Yarmouth's use of AEC buses was by no means exclusive over the years but is set to be the longest-lasting among local authority fleets, apart from preserved examples, for 12 Swift-model single-deckers are still in service in 1992. (Ivan Gould collection)

factory probably seemed quite easily unimportant at first, for its products were already entering service in growing numbers with LGOC, and bearing that concern's name, a practice which did not alter at first. Indeed AEC vehicles built for LGOC and, later, London Transport, continued to display the operator's name or initials on the radiator. However, the possibilities of supplying AEC-built chassis to other concerns had been seen, although B-types were at first supplied only in small numbers outside London.

As it turned out, an outcome from another merger of a London bus operator with LGOC was an arrangement with the Daimler Company in Coventry, making that concern agents for any AEC chassis surplus to LGOC requirements. There were to be later links with Daimler, but this first initiative had not been taken far before the outbreak of war in August 1914.

With AEC's experience in building vehicles in large numbers, it was understandable that authority was given for expanding the Walthamstow factory. The War Department's requirements were for a heavier-duty chassis and the resulting Y-type was turned out at a rate more than double that achieved with the B, making it

the most numerous of the British-built 3-tonners used by the armed services in the 1914-18 war. Production of what was in essence much the same model continued after the war, latterly being known as the 5-type. AEC's designations of that period were roughly related to the carrying capacity in tons and the Army's conservative rating translated into 5 tons.

Meanwhile, a new bus design – the K-type – was introduced for the LGOC in 1919. Its main new feature was the use of forward-control layout and while this in itself was not new, the half-cab arrangement that was to remain familiar on British buses for half a century was one of many instances of AEC pioneering over the years. The seating capacity went up to 46 but this was still not enough to meet LGOC's demand for buses that would carry more passengers, and the result was the S-type, similar in general design but longer and seating 54. Introduced at the end of 1920, it founded a new series of models known as the 4-types. A model numbering system was introduced, each series beginning at '01' and thus a new 2-ton model (AEC's only venture into so light a range) was 201, the relatively short-lived K was 301, and the S was 401 and the former Y became 501.

Later models in the various categories were designated with succeeding numbers, running up to 428 in the case of the 4-type family.

These various ranges were gradually developed during the 'twenties, though for the most part the basic design characteristics did not alter, with four-cylinder side-valve petrol engines of performance adequate for the very restrictive speed limitations of that period. There were innovations, most notably the NS double-decker, of similar size to the S but with a much lower-built frame made possible by the use of what in modern terms would be called a drop-centre double-reduction rear axle. The main aim when the prototype was built in 1923 was to obtain acceptance from the Metropolitan Police, who approved buses for use in the capital at that time, for a covered-top design by virtue of the lower build, but this was not permitted until 1926.

During the early 'twenties, AEC and Daimler had largely gone their separate ways and while AEC greatly expanded its sales of both passenger and goods chassis, Daimler's output of buses was relatively modest. There had been a Daimler Y-type lorry during the war, virtually identical to the AEC but for its sleeve-valve engine, but the Coventry firm did not

The uninitiated bystander would have had some difficulty in identifying the make, let alone the model, of this single-decker, for in the latter part of the Associated Daimler period the 'anonymous' radiator style shown had been adopted, although its affinity in general outline to that of contemporary Daimler cars would have been pretty obvious at the time. In fact, however, it was the first example of a new model and had the first engine of a design set to put new life into AEC. This was AEC Reliance chassis 660001 of late 1928, with A130 engine number 1 and a 32-seat bus body by Harrington, painted and lettered to suit a period of operation with the National Omnibus & Transport Co Ltd at its Weymouth garage, for whom it was registered in Dorset as TK 1662. The Reliance was, effectively, the ADC426 model chassis with John Rackham's new overhead-camshaft six-cylinder 6.1-litre engine and this example, like the other first few chassis, retained the 'plain' radiator AEC had inherited from ADC, rather than the version with triangle badge superimposed used on most Reliance models. However, the sharp-eyed would note the slightly-increased forward projection of the radiator to accommodate the larger engine, and when it moved off the smooth sound of a 6-type petrol engine would have been evident, albeit masked by the 'vintage' gearbox sounds from the old-style chassis – this particular one was actually rebuilt from 426018. National chose not to keep it and in 1929 it was sold to J. Sharp of Manchester.   (AEC)

continue with goods vehicle sales.

In 1926, there was a partial merger between AEC and the commercial-vehicle side of Daimler (the latter's main interest being in high-grade private cars). A joint sales company, the Associated Daimler Co Ltd, was set up and henceforth the vehicles involved were to be known by that name, often abbreviated to ADC. This was linked to AEC's new factory then in course of construction at Southall, Middlesex, on the western outskirts of London, where the administrative headquarters building carried the Associated Daimler name whereas the Associated Equipment title appeared on the production office frontage.

In practice, almost all ADC vehicles were of AEC manufacture, but in many of the 4-type passenger models a choice of engine was offered, there being a Daimler six-cylinder sleeve-valve option to the AEC four-cylinder side-valve unit (though even the latter now bore ADC nameplates).

This arrangement lasted for two years, but before long strains in the relationship between the two parent companies became evident. The Chairman of ADC was Lord Ashfield but the Chief Engineer was a Daimler appointee, Laurence Pomeroy, a notable engineer with his own views while Charles Edwards, designer of the NS, continued as AEC Chief

Engineer, working on a new six-wheel double-decker for the LGOC, designated by them as LS but with AEC model number 802. Daimler decided to 'go it alone' to some degree, with a new pair of single-deckers designed and built at Coventry and given the ADC model numbers 423 and 424 (forward- and normal-control respectively). At Southall, the radiator style – distinctly Daimler-like, but without the fluted finish used on Daimler cars of the period – was grafted on to the existing 416 and 417 single-deckers which became 426 and 427, retaining the AEC-type engine. But by then the whole thing was unravelling and in mid-1928, the two firms went their separate ways, and Southall-built chassis reverted to the AEC name.

The Rackham era

Lord Ashfield was able to give an up-beat tone to the announcement in July 1928 of the ending of the ADC exercise by also reporting the appointment of George John Rackham as Chief Engineer of AEC. His first job as an adult had been as a draughtsman with Vanguard in 1906 and he had been involved in the design of the X and B types, becoming AEC's first chief draughtsman on its formation in 1912. From 1916, his career took him elsewhere for a time,

including a spell on tank design for the War Office, and then in 1922, four years in the United States as Chief Engineer of the Yellow Coach Manufacturing Co Ltd, the predecessor of the General Motors bus plant. In 1926 he returned to England to take the equivalent post with Leyland Motors Ltd, in both of these being responsible for innovative bus designs.

His brief spell with Leyland was remarkably productive, for he was responsible for the original and highly successful Titan TD1 double-decker with a new six-cylinder overhead-camshaft engine and a completely fresh chassis design which set the pattern for virtually all makes of British double-decker for over 30 years. Lord Ashfield, whose own career had included a spell in the United States, kept in touch and actually ran a Rackham-designed Yellow Coach single-decker as a 'parlour coach'. It was said that Rackham found the rainy Lancashire climate not to his taste, but he may have been more influenced by an allegedly high salary and, perhaps even more, an indication of considerable freedom of action.

Action there certainly was, for a new engine was running in prototype form by September. Admittedly it closely resembled the Leyland engine Rackham had produced, though a

An important double-milestone in the evolution of the British motor bus is conveyed by this photograph taken in Glasgow in 1930, soon after the Corporation of that city had taken delivery of its first 25 Regent chassis. One – number 256 – is following the Austin six-cylinder car towards the camera, while two of the municipal undertaking's already large fleet of Leyland Titan TD1 models can also be seen – number 84 behind the Regent and 63 beyond 'standard' tram 473, both of these buses having the standard Leyland open-staircase body and dating from 1928. The Regent had Cowieson bodywork of the style standardised by Glasgow in 1930-31 – originally the chassis, like the rest of Glasgow's first nine, had the A136 6.1-litre petrol engine usual on early production Regents but the entire batch was converted to the 110mm bore 7.4-litre A145 unit quite early in life. (AEC)

fresh design with some new features and producing much the same power from slightly smaller capacity of 6.1-litres. As a stop-gap, it was installed in what amounted to the existing 426 chassis with no more than minor changes, the resulting model being given the type number 660 in a new system which indicated the number of cylinders as the second digit, and being given the name Reliance. The first examples went to operators late in 1928 but already work was in hand on a new chassis worthy of the engine.

This was the original Regent, model 661, of which a dozen prototype chassis had been bodied and delivered to operators by mid-1929. It too followed the general principles of the Titan design but a particularly neat front-end design both economised on space and gave a clean appearance which, again, set new standards for others to follow – within a few years what could reasonably be described as the Regent look had been copied to varying degrees by such other makes as Daimler, Dennis, Bristol, Crossley, Thornycroft and, from 1933, Leyland.

The corresponding single-deck Regal, type 662, soon followed, as did six-wheel 663 and 664 versions given the model name Renown, and a bonneted model, the Ranger, type 665.

Rackham was unenthusiastic about six-wheel buses, producing the Renown in response to LGOC request, yet the design was to prove very successful in London service, unlike most earlier six-wheel bus designs of various makes, partly because of design features intended to minimise stress and wear, notably the use of a third differential between the two driven axles. Amid all the uncertainties of the late 'twenties there had been moves for LGOC to design its own vehicles, a series of prototypes being built, but the Regent, Regal and Renown, respectively designated ST, T, and LT by LGOC, effectively put an end to such ideas. The Regent, in particular, attracted many orders from the municipal fleets in other cities and towns, in many cases beginning long spells of large-scale use of AEC products in places like Nottingham, Halifax and, a little later, Leeds.

The modernisation of the goods range was not forgotten and, indeed, from the beginning, Rackham planned his new 6-type range to use as many common components as possible, thus simplifying both manufacture and servicing. There were new six-cylinder goods models continuing the series of model numbers, 666 being the Majestic bonneted 6-tonner and the Mammoth forward-control 8-tonner, both of these having a larger-bore 7.4-litre version of the overhead camshaft engine also offered in – and later standardised for – passenger models.

It was realised that not everyone would want a six-cylinder engine, especially for lighter duty, and an equivalent four-cylinder range at first comprised the Mercury 640 bonneted 3½ ton model and the Monarch 641 forward-control 4-tonner. All these new goods models as well as the passenger types were included in the complete new range offered from October 1929, a quite astonishing achievement in only fifteen months from the announcement of Rackham's appointment.

But it didn't stop there, even though the new models were being built in vast numbers – the LGOC alone running over 2,500 by the end of 1932, if one includes some of the T-type coaches run by Green Line, then a separate company. In addition to further permutations of largely existing units, such as the four-cylinder 642-type Regal 4 single-deckers, and the six-wheel Mammoth Major 668, there were also various detail improvements to the existing range including slightly longer Regal

The complete new range of passenger and goods models introduced in 1929 included the original Mercury 640 model, a four-cylinder goods chassis, at first offered only in bonneted form. This is a 1932 example, with van body by Dickens of Loughborough, for the makers of the Sanatogen health beverage, based in the same town. (AEC)

and Regent models, the latter designated STL by the LGOC. But more fundamental work was going on.

AEC had been experimenting with what was then almost always called the oil engine in Britain since 1928, a prototype unit being fitted in one of the 802-type six-wheelers used to provide transport for workers living near Walthamstow across London to Southall, in November of that year. Another talented engineer, C. B. Dicksee was appointed to oversee oil engine development and a new 8-litre unit was developed and announced as a production option later in 1930, though this early design revealed a

need for further development.

The Ricardo concern of consultants was brought into the work and the revised 8.8-litre engine with a new combustion system patented by Ricardo proved both powerful, offering 130 bhp – a figure not exceeded in a British production road transport engine until after the 1939-45 war – and sufficiently reliable for a large-scale conversion to be put in hand for the London fleet of LT-class double-deckers on which much of the development work had been tried out in smaller-scale installations.

There was also an effort to improve vehicle transmission to give more durability in heavy traffic as well as

easier driving. The early 6-type models had a simple sliding-mesh four-speed gearbox but a version with constant-mesh engagement for third gear was introduced, at first for the LGOC, from 1931. More radically, the Daimler concern had introduced a combination of a fluid coupling – which they christened the fluid flywheel – with a preselective epicyclic gearbox invented by Walter Gordon Wilson, an engineer whom Rackham had known since the days when they both worked in tank design. The LGOC placed three Daimler buses so equipped in service and the outcome was a deal in which AEC could offer this form of transmission

Although much of the early work on AEC oil engines was related to bus applications, goods-vehicles were not forgotten. The first model to bear the Matador name was introduced as a four-cylinder 5-ton model in 1931, petrol-engined as standard at first, but this example dating from 1933, according to its registration number, was an early example to have the four-cylinder oil engine by then available, in all probability an A168 unit of 6.6-litre capacity. It was another instance of a vehicle with body built locally to the operator's base, the cab and drop-side body being by Goddard of Oadby, near Leicester. (Goddard)

The Q-type represented an immense leap into the future in design terms, and indeed too much for the operating industry of almost 60 years ago to accept, generally speaking. This view of Bradford Corporation's example, on chassis 761008, was taken very soon after it entered service in the late summer of 1933. It had what could be described as the standard Q double-deck body, built by Metro-Cammell but based on AEC's registered design as devised by John Rackham, accounting for roundly half the production (if the prototype, which differed in detail design, a lowbridge version for Birkenhead and two with minor modifications for London Transport are included). Yet these added up to merely a dozen, and only a total 23 of the 761-type double-deck chassis were built. Note the three-wheeler van, thought to be a James, and the West Yorkshire Road Car Co Leyland Lion PLSC bus, only about five years older than the Q but looking as if it belonged to a completely different era. (AEC)

on its vehicles from 1932. Again, early work was carried out on LT-class AEC Renown models.

A remarkable, if less successful venture was the side-engined Q-type passenger model first seen in 1932. The double-deck version, with entrance ahead of the front axle, had a layout remarkably like double-deckers of today – and indeed it could be said to have been a little too far ahead of its time and had only limited success.

The formation of the London Passenger Transport Board to take over the Underground group, as well as all other public transport undertakings operating in London except for the main-line railways, beginning in July 1933, caused AEC to be set up as an independent company. An agreement was made under which AEC continued to be the major supplier of motor buses to the new organisation, which adopted the fleetname London Transport in 1934. In practice, close liaison continued.

The LPTB decided on the STL-class Regent as its standard double-decker, settling on a new, more compact, 7.7-litre oil engine originally developed for the Q, with fluid transmission, as AEC generally described the fluid flywheel and Wilson preselective gearbox – over 2,000 of this combination had been

built by 1939. The oil-engined Regent was also favoured in such cities as Liverpool, Sheffield and Glasgow as well as those already mentioned. Company bus users of Regal and Regent models included several in the BET group in England and Wales and SMT in Scotland.

Another innovative venture which caught the public imagination in 1933 was the introduction of a streamlined railcar for the Great Western Railway, which steadily built up a fleet of such units.

AEC was the first manufacturer to introduce an oil or petrol-engined rigid eight-wheeler, this version of the Mammoth Major appearing in 1934 as model 680. There was also a new Matador model in 1931, this first bearer of the name, type 645, being a 5-ton forward-control four-cylinder model.

In 1935, however, the goods range was completely updated, the new Mark II models being slightly lighter to suit new legislation. The Monarch and Matador were now respectively four- and six-cylinder versions of the two-axle model (type numbers 344 or 346 or 244/246 if normal-control) while the Mammoth Major six- and eight-wheelers were 366 and 386 respectively. From about 1933 a prefix O was applied to oil-engined models, passenger or goods, these being in the

majority from the mid-'thirties, with the 7.7-litre as the standard six-cylinder, though the 8.8 continued to be available, and Gardner oil engines were also fitted to special order for a few customers.

Though there was a brief venture with a smaller six-cylinder oil engine, the so-called 6.6-litre, offered in the Regal Mark II O862 chassis from late 1935, London Transport was coming to the view that a large-capacity engine had advantage in terms of greater durability. There was also growing interest in air-pressure brake operation in place of the then usual vacuum servo.

This last was partly a spin-off from trolleybus practice, then of growing importance. AEC had built limited numbers of trolleybus chassis derived from its petrol models since the early 'twenties, following up with versions based on the Rackham-designed passenger range and designated 661T, 662T, etc. A joint sales arrangement with the English Electric Co Ltd led to them being marketed as AEC-English Electric, but in fact other makes of motors and electrical equipment were fitted in many cases to meet operators' preferences. Trolleybus sales were on a fairly modest scale until the mid-'thirties when London Transport began to replace trams with trolleybuses on quite a big scale. The

orders for vehicles for this were divided between AEC and Leyland on a roughly equal basis, and over 600 of the 664T six-wheel double-deckers had been supplied when production was halted by the 1939-45 war. There were also some sizeable municipal fleets.

An indication of the trend of development was London Transport's reversion to the 8.8-litre engine for a major renewal programme for the Green Line fleet comprising 266 AEC Regal coaches supplied in 1938 after earlier Green Line and other single-deck deliveries of both Q-type and Regal chassis in 1935-37 had specified

the 7.7. Moreover the new Green Line vehicles, and also a further batch of 8.8-litre engines which almost completed conversion of LT-class six-wheel Renown double-deckers, were of a new direct-injection type based on a similar pot-cavity design to that used by Leyland, giving better economy and very smooth running although not so much power as the Ricardo head. Meanwhile AEC had been working on a different, toroidal-cavity, direct-injection system which gave greater efficiency still, though at the cost of some loss of smoothness and this had gone into production, on a limited scale at first, from 1936 in

7.7-litre A173 form, though also offered later for the 8.8. By 1939, the A173 engine was the standard engine across the entire range, except for four-cylinder models or the Regal Mark II.

London Transport decided to adopt the philosophy of the larger pot-cavity engine, eventually deciding on 9.6-litre capacity for a new design of double-decker, together with air-pressure operation for the brakes and preselective gearbox. A new chassis design with many other new features was produced and emerged with a new design of body built by LT at its Chiswick works (as had been standard

Possibly the strangest-looking of AEC's goods models of the late 'thirties was the Mammoth Minor, giving the impression that someone had forgotten to fit a pair of outer wheels and tyres on the rearmost axle. At about that time a demand had arisen for a model with weight capacity between that of the two-axle Matador and the conventional six-wheel Mammoth Major. Other manufacturers produced the twin-steer type of six-wheeler to meet this need, but AEC did not favour the idea (until much later, when Maudslay had shown that there was a market for such a vehicle). Hence the Mammoth Minor with single-tyred rearmost trailing axle. This example, with 1939 registration, was run by a Birmingham operator, being seen in early wartime, when only one masked headlamp was permitted to be used, though the missing right-hand unit, with wiring still exposed, looks almost as if it might have been a case of wartime theft. The deeper radiator by then standard modernised the appearance considerably. (AEC)

practice going back to LGOC days) as RT1 in 1939. Further batches of RT-type Regents were ordered but only 150 of these were built, mostly entering service in 1940-41, before the war put a stop to production. These vehicles again set new standards, and as well as laying down the character of the typical London bus that was to continue until the 'sixties and not disappear from the capital's streets until 1979, they were to set trends accepted far more widely.

AEC at war

The Mark II goods range continued in production up to the war with little change apart from the addition of a Mammoth Minor model, this being a lighter-duty six-wheeler with single-tyred trailing axle at the rear. However, as the threat of war increased, military variants on the goods range as well as purely military products grew in variety as well as volume. There had been an AEC version of a military specification 6 x 4 model with four-cylinder petrol engine and canvas-topped cab since 1931, this being the Marshal, and larger numbers were built from 1938. Co-operation with a small concern in Slough called Hardy Motors Ltd, involved in all-wheel-drive vehicles (and also the railcars already mentioned), had led to absorption by AEC and to the evolution of what was

to become one of its most famous products, a four-wheel-drive military vehicle.

This was the O853 model, to which the Matador name, already in use for civilian four-wheel goods models using basically the same 7.7-litre direct-injection engine, was applied. As the numbers built grew far beyond those of the civilian model, 'Matador' began to be identified with the military vehicle and although a civilian Matador reappeared briefly again after the war, AEC eventually gave in to the pressure of common parlance and abandoned the name for anything but the 4 x 4 military vehicle. Officially, the O853 was intended as a medium artillery tractor, but was used for a wide variety of purposes. Its quality can be judged by the German Army's comment that it was the best tractor in either army during the North African campaign. Some 9,620 were built when military contracts ceased in November 1945, though the model remained available and was built in small quantities until the early 'fifties.

There were other military models, notably the 854 which could broadly be described as a 6 x 6 equivalent to the Matador using a Marshal-type rear bogie though the Royal Air Force, by whom it was chosen as an aircraft refuelling tanker, required petrol engines at first, probably to simplify fuel requirements on the bomber stations to which they were allocated.

Some 1,500 were built from 1940, many in great urgency as their 2,500-gallon capacity was needed to allow the huge numbers of four-engined bombers, whose tanks could each carry nearly as much, to be refuelled quickly.

There were also armoured cars of two series and engines (which had been supplied for a variety of uses, including marine, since the early days of AEC oil engines) were produced both for use in tanks and other makers' vehicles. Normal civilian deliveries were limited from the beginning of the war and stopped entirely in 1942 though from 1943 AEC 7.7-litre engines were supplied to Daimler and, later, Bristol for use in utility bus chassis and similarly to ERF and Maudslay for goods models.

Normality began to return with the ending of the war in 1945, with chassis very like the standard models as they stood in 1942, with 7.7-litre engines and crash gearboxes and no alternatives in either respect. The Regent in this form became the Regent II but the Regal was called Regal I after it was remembered that there had already been a Mark II. The two-axle goods models were designated Monarch if intended for solo operation but Matador as a machine equipped to draw a two-axle trailer, both now having the 7.7 engine. However, the 9.6-litre engine, now with toroidal direct injection, was adopted as the

The wartime Matador O853 was intended primarily as an artillery tractor although put to numerous other uses in wartime and ever since. This example, in post-war gloss paint and towing a 5.5in. gun was representing the 58th Med. Regt., Royal Artillery, "A" Sub, at the Kings Birthday parade in Nathan Road, Kowloon, Hong Kong on 7th June 1951. The photograph was supplied by Ken Marriott.

The Royal Air Force was also a Matador user – this one with platform body is seen after towing a Short Sunderland flying boat of 88 Squadron, weighing some 20 tons, out of the water for servicing in Kai-Tak, Hong Kong in November 1947. The photograph was taken by Jim Muncie, then a Sergeant in the RAF. This location became the site of Hong Kong International Airport.

The Regal I, type 0662/20, was AEC's immediate post-war single-deck standard. By 1946 the extensively louvred bonnet was a rather old-fashioned feature, as well as a rather surprising one as in 1938-39 oil-engined AEC passenger models had 'plain' bonnet panels as standard, giving a more up-to-date look. This example from a batch with Duple A-type (FS1) bodywork for the Grey-Green fleet was quite an early example of a post-war Regal with coach body. The recently introduced Corgi model of a Regal coach is in some respects closer to this design than the Regal III, especially as at first introduced with louvred bonnet, even though the layout of louvres is incorrect. (Duple)

Exports were regarded as the key to rebuilding Britain's prosperity after the war and AEC played its full part. The left-hand Regal III O963 and related models outsold the right-hand O962, the latter itself with substantial export sales. The decision was made to design a properly 'handed' model, not only with left-hand steering but the whole chassis and the units within it, most notably the engine, laid out to give as good accessibility as the versions with right-hand steering – always a strong AEC characteristic. It paid off, not least in the case of Lisbon, when the CCFL fleet was to remain faithful to Regal and Regent chassis almost to the end of the Mark V era, and helped to foster a much wider market, one of the company's strongest, in Portugal generally. One of 32 Regal III models with Weymann bodywork dating from 1948 is seen being shipped.

power unit for the Mammoth Major six- and eight-wheelers.

New Mark III models for a new world

There was a feeling of expansiveness after the austerity of war and although material shortages continued to be a problem, AEC's new Mark III passenger and goods ranges were in tune with the times. The Regent III was based on the RT, itself modified in detail to become the main basis of London Transport's plans for fleet renewal, expanded because of the scarcity of new vehicles during the war and the subsequent decision to replace the remaining London trams with motor buses – some 4,674 were

built in the period up to 1954. The so-called 'provincial' Regent III and the corresponding Regal III single-decker had the same main features of the 9.6-litre engine and air-operated pre-selective gearbox and brakes as standard but did not have the RT's distinctive low bonnet line. Versions with the familiar crash gearbox and also the 7.7-litre engine (offered with crash box only) were added to meet some operators' preferences.

Exports had become very important to help rebuild the national economy and AEC played its full part. There had been a useful minority of overseas sales in pre-war days, when those for South America were sold under the ACLO name from the mid-'twenties, after a dispute with

the German AEG electrical concern. As part of a drive to build up business in countries where left-hand steering was standard a complete redesign of the Regal III to produce what was virtually a mirror-image chassis was carried out. Not only were the steering and other controls on the left but the engine was itself built in opposite-hand form and the transmission re-aligned to suit. South America was a particular target for this and other models, and left-hand drive models of this period had Spanish lettering as standard because of this, although the language was changed if necessary, of course.

The Mark III goods range introduced in 1947 looked outwardly very like late Mark II models with the same elegant design of standard cab – a typical manifestation of Rackham interest in such matters. Although AEC did not build cabs, bodybuilders were supplied with drawings indicating the favoured design and although some operators chose different styles, it was very widely used. The 9.6-litre engine was now standard for all models except the Monarch and it was in 1951 that AEC decided to drop the use of Matador as a name for its two-axle general-duty goods model which was given the name Mandator previously used for a rare low-floor goods model in the early 'thirties. Other features common to these larger-engined types were a new five-speed constant-mesh gearbox and air-pressure brakes. Gradually other British makers of the heavier commercial vehicles began to offer air brakes, but AEC was the first to regard them as standard over the majority of its products.

Trolleybus and railcar production was transferred to a new joint enterprise with Leyland called British United Traction Ltd, or BUT. Chassis of AEC design continued to be built but the trolleybus was past its peak in Britain – the association with Leyland went no further at that stage.

What could be called the Mark III era continued to the mid-'fifties, for passenger models and the early 'sixties for goods and AEC, like many other makers, turned out immense numbers of vehicles to meet the world-wide demand after the wartime years of shortage – over 8,000 Regent III models, including the RT-type, and 6,293 Mammoth Major III six- and eight-wheelers. There were some

changes in that time, such as the introduction of an 11.3-litre larger-bore derivation of the 9.6-litre engine, directly interchangeable where more power was needed and increasingly common for the heavier goods models as the years went by.

There had been an awareness of growing interest in underfloor-engined passenger models since 1939, when AEC built a prototype chassis with 9.6-litre engine for Canada. Work

on the project was resumed in 1946 and by the beginning of 1949 the first prototype of a new model, the Regal IV, had been bodied. The mechanical features were basically similar to those of the standard Mark III passenger models, with 9.6-litre engine, air-operated preselective gearbox and brakes. The main user was once again London Transport, for whom 700 were built to form the RF class, subdivided into coaches,

both for Green Line and other duties, and bus for Central Area (red) and Country Area (green) fleets, delivery being made in 1951-53. Total orders amounted to over 1,900, most going overseas in the period up to 1960, though home market sales virtually ceased by 1955.

This was also a period of enlargement of the AEC empire with take-overs of Crossley and Maudslay on the chassis side and Park Royal

(which had itself acquired the Leeds firm, Roe) among bodybuilders. The parent company was retitled Associated Commercial Vehicles Ltd to embrace its new character but the Southall factory and its products were put under a new company, AEC Ltd, from 1948.

The British involvement in the Korean war brought an upsurge of interest in military vehicles and two new models, the O859 and O860, respectively of 6 x 4 and 6 x 6 type, appeared in 1952, being given the name Militant. The main user was the Army but examples were built for other users and over 3,000 had been built by the early 'sixties.

The medium weights

G. J. Rackham retired in 1950, and although his philosophy remained strongly evident at AEC for several years, changes in market needs combined with changes in management style gradually emerged. The immediate post-war surge in demand was dying away in the early 'fifties and expansion of the range into a lighter category was in tune with renewed interest in operating costs – the Mark III and Mark IV passenger models in particular were appreciably heavier than their predecessors, partly because of increased dimensions then permissible.

A new range officially described as mediumweights and having the letter M in their type designations was put in hand, largely the brain-children of Bob Fryars, Assistant Chief Engineer at the time, the initial models being the Mercury, reviving the name of the early 'thirties model bearing a similar relationship to the AEC range of that period, and a pair of underfloor-engined passenger models, the Reliance (again reviving an old name) and the Monocoach. The last-mentioned was, despite its name, an integral-construction bus. They had alternative new engines designated AV410 or AV470 in vertical form and of $6\frac{3}{4}$ and $7\frac{3}{4}$ litres capacity respectively – the horizontal versions for the passenger chassis were AH410 and AH470. They were developed from the pre-war Regal Mark II engine and had wet-liner construction. It was claimed that difficulties experienced with this had been overcome, and the new models attracted many new as well as existing AEC customers, offering quite lively performance by contemporary standards, especially with the larger engine (which soon became standard), aided by the five-speed synchromesh gearbox.

A synchromesh option had been offered on Mark III and IV passenger models from 1952 and for a time there was a growing tendency for operators to favour this, though London Transport and some other city fleets remained faithful to fluid transmission. AEC's double-deck range took on a three-way split at this time, something which Rackham would surely have resisted. On the one hand there was some pressure in favour of a lighter double-decker with AH470 engine having some of the characteristics of the Reliance, though it has to be said that Bob Fryars was not very enthusiastic about double-deckers in general. Such a model did appear, being publicised as the main innovation of the new Regent V range introduced in 1954 though 9.6-litre versions continued, retaining many characteristics of the Regent III, and in the long run greatly outnumbered the lighter type.

What had been the traditional line of development for AEC going back to its early days – involvement in London bus design and construction – was represented by London Transport's project for a new generation of double-decker. This was to be the successor to the highly-regarded RT, by no means an easy act to follow. London Transport's Chief Mechanical Engineer (Road Services) was A. A. M. Durrant, whose vision had been responsible for the RT and, indeed, influenced the major part of the STL fleet. Here, too, there was an awareness of weight and the cost of

The Mercury name was revived in 1953 for a new range of mediumweight goods models which appeared at a time when there was a growing demand for such a vehicle, built to more robust standards than available from the mass producers yet lighter, more nimble and less costly than the traditional heavy-duty category. Sales success was almost immediate and the Mercury was to have a key role in the AEC story from then until the end of production. Early-generation examples had several minor variations of standard cab design but the rounded nose projection ahead of the windscreen line was characteristic. The grille, wider than the traditional radiator with the triangle badge on a localised plinth rather than inset into the curves of the main outline, was to be used on many subsequent models, passenger as well as goods. This smart-looking example with BTC four-in-line trailer dates from 1957 and is still in use by Michael McGeehan, of Draperstown, County Derry, Northern Ireland – it must qualify as one of the oldest AEC models still on haulage duties in the United Kingdom. (M. McGeehan)

continually accelerating and braking every superfluous pound. On the other hand, the sacrifice of passenger comfort was ruled out and indeed improvements on both this and ease of driving were regarded as equally important.

The result was the Routemaster, developed as a joint exercise by LT, AEC and Park Royal, for it was to be of integral construction with widespread use of aluminium alloy for the framing. Although the traditional half-cab rear-entrance layout was to be retained, the mechanical specification was in advance of any comparable vehicle, with independent front suspension and power hydraulic brakes as key features. The 9.6-litre engine and the basic principle of the Wilson gearbox was retained, though the latter progressed through the no-clutch-pedal direct selection form to fully automatic. A 64-seat capacity was chosen as a compromise between the traditional 56 and the 70 of London trolleybuses, for replacement of the latter was in mind. The first prototype appeared in 1954 and three others followed, two with Leyland units and body structure by ECW and Weymann respectively, but the AEC-Park Royal combination won the day.

Another strand of thought was instigated by A. J. Romer, AEC's Managing Director, who was appointed in August 1950, just after Rackham's retirement. He was an engineer, having been with the Bristol concern previously and involved with the Lodekka low-floor double-decker. A similar project was decided upon for AEC, the result being christened the Bridgemaster and having a somewhat similar layout to the Lodekka, though the vehicle was of integral construction and was also a joint project with Park Royal. The actual development work was entrusted to Crossley, with the prototype appearing at the 1956 Commercial Motor Show.

In the event, an unexpected fall-off in London's bus needs, as the demand for bus travel fell, delayed the beginning of Routemaster production until the latter part of 1958 and Bridgemaster orders proved fewer than had been hoped, so most double-deck output tended to remain with the Regent. Fortunately demand for the Mercury and Reliance was strong, and even the venerable Mark III goods range continued to attract plenty of custom. This too moved to a Mark V series, with sleek-looking cab design, first seen in 1959, though there was an overlap of a couple of years or so before the old model was phased out. A replacement engine design, retaining the 9.6/11.3-litre size but with similar wet-liner monobloc construction to the smaller units,

appeared as the AV590/690 and was fitted to Mark V goods and production Routemasters, though the left-hand 11.3-litre remained in production for export passenger requirements, notably those for Baghdad, Lisbon and Tehran, from all of which sizeable orders for Regent V models were received in the later 'fifties and into the 'sixties.

Sales of the goods vehicles in particular were increasing during this period, and both Mercury and Mandator models found wider use as articulated tractor units as the general popularity of such vehicles increased. In one sense, this shift of emphasis was just as well, for pressure on space was becoming a growing problem at Southall, and it was possible to get more short-wheelbase chassis into the available production line capacity.

Further new models were added to the range and a fresh line of development was the dump truck. The first step had been the beefing up of basically standard Mammoth Major III six-wheelers as heavy-duty tippers for off-road duty, graduating into a dump-truck version and then the introduction of a much larger vehicle on the pattern of American-built machines. This was the 1100 Dumptruk, with a special AEC-built 18-litre engine, the AV1100, not used in any other AEC road vehicle. However, it did find a use in horizontal

This photograph might well have been taken to mark the delivery of the Mammoth Major Mark V when new in 1961 to Alan Firmin Transport Ltd of Linton, Kent. In fact it was taken last year by Peter Davies for *Trucking International* after a two-year restoration. It had been retired in 1971 after clocking about 70,000 miles a year, often at maximum weight and with a drawbar trailer – for a long period making regular trips to Scotland. It was cut down to make a 6 x 4 recovery vehicle and Bob Willard, who had been appointed its driver when it was new, rising to become Transport Manager, persuaded the firm to restore it. The task was entrusted to Dave Hayward who has also worked for the firm, again originally as a driver, since 1964 but is now workshop foreman – the result has been plated and tested but is set for a more relaxed life visiting rallies and shows up and down the country.

form in railcars, though the peak years of AEC involvement in these was when British Railways was greatly expanding its diesel multiple unit fleet in the change-over from steam during the late 'fifties and the horizontal AEC 11.3-litre engine shared with the equivalent Leyland O.680 unit in the supply of engines for these vehicles.

Reverting to more conventional goods vehicles, mention should be made of the reintroduction of Monarch as a model name for export versions of the Mercury and later the revival of Marshal for a three-axle general haulage model to suit a need for a lighter vehicle than the Mammoth Major, based on Mercury-range components. Old Maudslay names were revived, notably Mogul for a new bonneted two-axle export goods type contemporary with the Mark V forward-control models, although the six-wheel equivalent was called Majestic. Another Maudslay name was Mustang, appropriately used for a twin-steer six-wheeler which was another model based on Mercury range parts.

In 1961, the ACV group's final additional company made its appearance with the takeover of the Thornycroft goods vehicle business, with its factory at Basingstoke. That

concern's home-market range, which sold only in limited numbers, was dropped, but its specialist models, notably the Nubian fire crash tender and, for a while, the Trusty and Big Ben bonneted overseas models, continued. However, both the Maudslay and Thornycroft factories were given an important role in the manufacture of AEC vehicles, becoming effectively the firm's axle and gearbox factories.

Merger and decline

In 1962, the management of both AEC and Leyland were conscious of increasing competition from foreign manufacturers for overseas business. Each concern was spending considerable sums in maintaining a sales organisation and submitting tenders for possible contracts and it was considered that it would be sensible for there to be a complete merger, and the agreement for this was announced on 5th June 1962. In theory, the Leyland group as it had stood immediately before this (including Albion, Scammell and the Standard-Triumph car concern) would remain separate from ACV in the home market, but the two were henceforth to co-operate in seeking

export orders. In fact, Leyland's dominance, both as the larger partner and in terms of management personalities, was soon to become evident with Donald (later Lord) Stokes, who had built his career on successes in world sales of Leyland buses in particular, emerging as Chairman of AEC as well as the whole group.

For the first few years no change in policy was evident to the outside world. On the passenger side, AEC enjoyed fresh success with its 36ft.-long version of the Reliance, with AH590 engine and six-speed ZF synchromesh gearbox, which proved almost ideally suited to motorway work with its 70mph cruising capability. Almost immediately after the merger, a new low-floor double-deck chassis was announced, the Renown (yet another revival of an old name), intended to take over from the integral Bridgemaster, but its success was similarly rather limited. On the other hand, the Routemaster had been in full production since 1959 and was to continue until the last few of the London Transport total of 2,760 entered service early in 1968, the later ones classified RML to signify their 30ft. length as opposed to the standard RM's 27ft. 6in.

The Regent V was still doing well

with both home and, especially, export sales, but the days of big sales for front-engined double-deckers were coming to an end. AEC and London Transport co-operated in a venture to produce a rear-engined Routemaster, but the combination of LT's strong even if fairly short-lived enthusiasm for the possibilities of single-deckers (which were seen as having the advantage of being capable of driver-only operation, not at the time of the original plans legally permissible on a double-decker) plus Leyland management policy killed it off, and only one prototype, FRM1, was built.

To meet the new demand for 'city' single-deckers with a low floor line, the Leyland group introduced rear-engined models with common frame pressings and generally similar layout but distinctively Leyland or AEC units. The basic standard Leyland model was the Panther, with a lighter Panther Cub option. AEC's standard version fitted between these two in terms of engine size, with the AH505 8.2-litre engine – in effect a slightly enlarged AH470 also having 'dry'

cylinder liners in an effort to overcome a source of trouble with the 470, especially if driven hard. This vehicle was given the name Swift and a heavier-duty version was to be Merlin, but that name became associated specifically with the London Transport versions which had AH691 engines (the dry-liner equivalent of the AH690 11.3-litre unit which had been used in export markets in Regal VI models, successors to the Regal IV overseas versions).

Some 665 Merlin buses were built, but LT found that their 11-metre length made them too cumbersome for many London routes, so a switch was then made to 10-metre Swift models, of which 838 were supplied up to 1972. By then, LT had decided that double-deckers were, after all, the best bet for most of its routes but the business went to Daimler, by then an associated company, with the Fleetline model, and AEC ceased to be 'the maker of London's buses' after some 60 years as the principal supplier. The manufacture of AEC double-deckers faded out in the late 'sixties – perhaps

appropriately, models bearing the name Regent were the last to enter service – two of the mediumweight variety for Pontypridd in March 1969.

Meanwhile the goods range had altered completely in its visual design with the adoption of the Leyland Ergomatic tilt cab for forward-control models, beginning in 1964. However, it gave a misleading impression that the chassis had become 'Leylandised', for the same cab design was being used on contemporary Leyland models. This was not so, for they retained AEC mechanical design in almost all respects. The new dry-liner engines were standardised throughout the range – the AV471 replacing the AV470, though the AV505 was very widely used (and, incidentally, sold to other vehicle makers, such as Seddon) and the AV691 replacing both the AV590 and AV690, with a new, larger AV760 with 12.5-litre capacity, at the top of the vehicle range. AEC-designed gearboxes and axles also continued to be used.

The goods side of the business had grown in importance, both relatively

The underfloor-engined Reliance, successful from the beginning in its original 30ft. form with AH470 engine, grew and grew again as length regulations were relaxed and demand rose for longer vehicles. An important step was the availability of the ZF six-speed synchromesh gearbox with the AH590, and later the AH691, engine in the 11- and 12-metre chassis, making a vehicle that was able to take advantage of motorways at the 70mph limit at a time when most competitors had nothing directly comparable. Seen here is one of a pair of 12-metre Reliance 691 models with Plaxton Panorama Elite bodywork, like the variant of the chassis new at the time, that were exhibited at the 1968 Commercial Motor Show. This one seated 57 and was for Chiltern Queens – in gold lettering on the window is the quoted basic price of £3500 for the chassis and £5250 for the body – even allowing for inflation, what value! The unladen weight was 8 tons 9cwt. 3qr. – have we really advanced all that much since then? (AEC)

in relation to the decline of AEC's involvement with buses and also because the goods range suited a wide range of users' needs. It is significant that Bob Fryars, who had risen to become Chief Engineer of AEC, was appointed Chief Engineer of the combined group's Truck Division based at the engineering headquarters at Leyland. Increasingly, major design projects were handled at Leyland, leaving the Southall-based engineering staff to deal with more day-to-day matters such as tailoring vehicles to operators' individual requirements.

Then in 1968 came the merger of the Leyland group as it then stood with the huge but far from healthy British Motor Corporation, which brought in not only Austin, Morris, etc but also the smaller but much livelier if also underfunded Jaguar-Daimler-Guy group, making AEC part of an even wider conglomerate. As it happened, only ten days later came the announcement of what was described as the 'British Leyland 800-series' V8 engine, though in fact it would have been more honest in acknowledging its design origin to call it an AEC product. It was offered in a suitably adapted Mandator, making an impressively powerful vehicle with 250 bhp available from 12.1 litres without turbocharge.

Unfortunately the V8 was troublesome and, with vast resources being swallowed up by the ailing volume car side of the new British Leyland Motor Corporation empire, there was inadequate effort to cure its faults – vee-form engines are notoriously difficult to perfect though when 'right' they offer power in a compact form. Much the same, writ larger, was the problem with Leyland's whole commercial vehicle empire in which there was an immense combination of talent but insufficient resources to take advantage of it. Added to that, the manufacturing plants remote from Leyland suffered increasingly from a degree of bureaucracy which was understandable in a mass-production concern but not to one where many vehicles are tailor-made to some degree.

So AEC at Southall soldiered on into the 'seventies with the goods range plus the Reliance coach chassis – the Swift was killed off as Leyland sought to build up demand for the Leyland National – and in the last few years a visit to Southall was an increasingly depressing experience. There was a sense of decay about the place and it was clear that its days were numbered. A combination of factors worked against it – on the one hand there was no room for further expansion, because the sports field in the centre of the site was sacrosanct under planning controls, while on the other, skilled labour was increasingly being drawn away to the workshops associated with London Airport only a few miles away. In the process this pushed up local wage rates, making them uneconomic by comparison with those still applying in Lancashire or at the new Leyland National factory deliberately sited in an area near Workington where there was unemployment.

So it was no surprise when the end finally came on 25th May 1979, and the once-great Southall factory closed. Leyland preference for centralisation had 'won', but there were still echoes of earlier days. For example, BLMC's then new TL12 engine was really an updated AV760 and it was an intriguing detail of history that its stroke dimension, 142mm, had been common back down the decades not only to the AV760 but through the 'classic' Mark III 11.3- and 9.6-litre types and the pre-war 8.8-litre to AEC's first production oil engine, the 8.1-litre A155 engine of 1930. It was a clear indication of how each generation of design evolved from its predecessors, a good principle for a reliable product.

Few, if any, firms of comparable size had achieved so much in terms of leading trends of vehicle design, quite apart from building vehicles meant to give lasting service and, designed from the start with the operator's needs in terms of durability and straightforward maintenance very much in mind. No wonder so many survive.

"The last one. 1979. R.I.P." The scene on the production line at Southall as output ended has an atmosphere of irony as well as sadness. The vehicle, with temporary cab, is a Leyland Marathon, though someone had found AEC lettering and a blue triangle to adorn it, and of course the TL12 engine used in this model was a direct development of the AEC AH760, so it had technical as well as nostalgic justification. There was a wry note in some of the placards – one said "In the words of our leader, Mr Michael Edwards (then BLMC's boss) – self-financing productivity – CLOSE THEM!" But there was pride, too – the banner attached to the bumper read "AEC – we were the greatest". History, and the respect for the marque which seems to grow as the years go by, lends more than a little justification to the claim. (AEC)

While in a nostalgic mood, these views in and around the Southall works will bring memories back to those who worked or called there. This view was taken in June 1950 to show progress on the concrete hard standing being provided for 'the float', as the collection of chassis awaiting delivery or, in some cases, short of particular parts was known. The growth of exports and consequent relation to shipping dates had made more space essential, yet it was to remain common for chassis to be parked in odd spaces around the works in the mid-'fifties. Two

bonneted Mammoth Major left-hand chassis with cab tops on the frame to reduce shipping height can be seen, and two bodied Regal III coaches outside the chassis inspection department, that on the right having Duple full-fronted bodywork of a type built only in small numbers. Apart from an Austin A40, all the cars appear to be pre-war, and all British except for a Renault (though even that might have been assembled at Acton). Note the water tower, which had carried the AEC bulls-eye emblem in pre-war days, though not later. (AEC)

Southall scenes

This view dating from January 1954 was taken to show 'congested buildings', in other words the collection of sheds that had grown up, largely in wartime, in the middle of the works, housing a variety of activities and soon to be replaced. Alan Townsin, co-author of this book, should have been hard at work in the drawing office on the upper floor of the building in the background on the right, but well recalls the typical scene in the works yard to the left of the picture. Near the camera, two pre-war Mammoth Majors in the yellow and blue works transport fleet livery await the next job, such as collecting material, preferably

combined with delivery of spare units and parts. New chassis in delivery aluminium paint, some of them back from bodybuilders after receiving cabs, include some Militants as well as various Mark III goods and passenger models. Two Militants with cabs in Army green are also visible, as well as a complete Army Matador – it is possible that the latter was one of a batch which came in for some modifications around this period – Alan recalls that they were unusual in being petrol-engined, and remained so. The boiler chimneys are prominent in both these views. (AEC)

This view of the 'track' in January 1951 brings back vivid memories to co-author Alan Townsin, for although his job was in the drawing office when he joined the firm in September the same year, he always found it fascinating to see what was being built. In this scene, the leading vehicle is a Matador Mark III 3472 tractive unit – the change of name for this model to Mandator had yet to happen later that year – followed by some Regal IV chassis, which at that date were almost certainly from the first production batch of 9821LT chassis, of 27ft. 6in. length, for London Transport's RF private hire fleet. Delivery of the 25 chassis had begun in November and continued until early February.   (AEC)

The export of chassis in 'completely knocked-down' (CKD) form was becoming common practice in the 'fifties, often to meet requirements for local assembly to help foster the importing country's economic and employment interests. Here two Reliance chassis for Spitals, the AEC agency in Belgium, are seen in this form on a British Road Services trailer for delivery via that organisation's continental ferry service in January 1958. This was before the general adoption of containers, and the various units are seen grouped under the two frames mounted on wooden supports to give suitable room. A tarpaulin would have given weather protection and some safety from petty pilfering of small items, but there is little doubt that it was a more honest world in those days.   (AEC)

This view of one of the first AEC goods chassis to receive the Leyland group 'Ergomatic' tilt cab – probably one of the exhibits for the 1964 Show, or a demonstrator – is also likely to strike a nostalgic chord for anyone who worked in, or visited, the drawing office or experimental department at Southall. The door in the background marked 'no admittance' (to discourage prying eyes) was the entrance through which one went, upstairs to the D.O. – on the same upper floor were the offices of the chief engineer and his senior staff, whilst downstairs was the experimental department in which prototype chassis were built – and numerous other investigations of new ideas (or, indeed, cases of recurring faults on production models) were carried out. Again, there were offices for the experimental engineer and his assistants. Looking back, there can be little doubt that AEC was an engineer-led concern, especially in its most successful years. Maybe it was not for nothing that the chief engineer's department building was more impressive than the single-storey headquarters offices alongside.   (AEC)

More nostalgia for anyone interested in commercial vehicles who travelled on British Rail Western Region main line past AEC's works. This photograph was taken by the late E. J. Smith, from a train moving at about 20mph, on 16th March 1952. The big AEC logo sign, with the proud slogan 'Builders of London's Buses' is visible in the background – it was neon-lit at night. Most of the double-deckers visible, all Regent III models with Weymann bodywork, are left-hand 9631E models in grey primer for CCFL, Lisbon, part of the batch of 25 in course of delivery – several were to be seen around the factory for some months awaiting shipping. Nearest the camera is a 9613A with lowbridge body for South Wales Transport; also visible are two of the Regal III 9631A single-deckers with Park Royal bodywork for export to Baghdad and an AEC works lorry, probably a Monarch. Few bodied vehicles came back to Southall – final checks were generally carried out by the regional service depots.

The approaches to AEC in either direction along the Uxbridge road were signposted by large placards on the Iron Bridge carrying the Western Region (Great Western Railway, pre-1948) main line which runs obliquely over the road at this point and formed the boundary of the factory site further west. The view as one approached from central London after passing through Hanwell is seen on the right. A driver unused to the area had to be quite observant to notice the arrow, which was the only indication of direction on this side, especially as there was the traffic light protecting the junction at Windmill Lane to watch. The Routemaster, RM476, was new in November 1960, one of the allocation replacing trolleybuses based at Hanwell (HL) to work the 207 route which took over from the 607 trolleybus; the existence of the overhead wires indicates that the conversion had just taken place. Within a hundred yards or so it would pass what then became known as Southall garage, though that too had been Hanwell, as conveyed by its HW code, until renamed to avoid confusion.

In the opposite direction, the AEC sign was more explicit, the right turn then being as described – later it became necessary to run some distance towards Hanwell before being allowed to turn back, and then left into Windmill Lane. The vehicle turning into Greenford Road in this view is a brand new Reliance 590 with Harrington Grenadier body for Black & White Motorways Ltd of Cheltenham, almost certainly on a test run, judging by the boiler-suited driver – it may have called in an Southall on its way from the bodybuilders at Hove with some defect needing attention. The triangle badge for this operator was a special version in black with red AEC bullseye – the only other known colour variant of the standard monogram was Aldershot & District's green with cream centre used on its Reliances. (AEC)

HEAD OFFICES & WORKS
SOUTHALL, MIDDLESEX

(Opposite page) Comparison of these two aerial views of Southall works conveys how it developed over the years. The top view dates from about 1948 and is taken from the west, with the main line railway running along the top left of the picture and Windmill Lane across the top. The factory was not greatly changed from its original concept when built in 1926-27, though the series of larger buildings in the foreground had been added to provide more room, partly because of general expansion but also to cater for the greater complexity of vehicles and also diversification into such fields as railcars and trolleybuses. The service department occupied the premises in the top right of the picture, acting both as the depot for customers in the area and as headquarters for the chain of branches and agencies elsewhere in Britain and abroad. Looking back, a striking feature was the small proportion of office accommodation. The modest-sized single-storey building facing the row of poplar trees in the centre of the picture was the management and sales offices and there were offices for the production control and related activities occupying a small area of the main block of buildings (facing the area with the flagpole more readily visible in the later view, so often seen in official vehicle photographs) and very little else. The chief engineer's department (drawing office and experimental) was in the two-storey block alongside the management offices. Poplars also lined the drive and there was a conscious attempt to make the premises a pleasant place in which to work, with the green space of the sports field as part of the overall picture.

The lower view dates from 1962 and was probably taken firstly to mark the firm's 50th anniversary and also to record the impressive frontage along Windmill Lane (in the foreground of this view, taken from an almost opposite direction) that had just been completed with the construction of the new chassis inspection shop. The site was almost full, apart from the sports field (by then a designated 'green space') and indeed ultimately the lack of capability for further expansion was a factor which played its part in Leyland's decision to close the factory in 1979. Ironically, it would have been plenty large enough for much of the drastically curtailed heavy commercial vehicle industry of today. (AEC)

The preservation movement for commercial vehicles barely existed before about 1958 but, to the great good fortune of posterity, London Transport and its predecessors had a strong sense of history. Thus, when the Omnibus Society celebrated its silver jubilee in 1954, it was possible to hire four buses dating back to the period between 1910 and 1926. The oldest, B340, is seen passing through Piccadilly Circus on that occasion. Strictly speaking, this is not an AEC, for when it was built in 1910, the Associated Equipment Company had not been formed and it is thus correct to describe this vehicle and other early B-types as an LGOC, for the Walthamstow works in which its chassis was built was then owned by and operated as a department of the London General Omnibus Co Ltd. (E. J. Smith)

Walthamstow warriors

If the B-type represented AEC's beginning, the expansion to build the Y-type in previously unequalled quantities during the 1914-8 war made the firm the largest British maker of heavy-duty commercial vehicles of that period by a wide margin. This one was built for Army service in 1917 but in 1924 became a charabanc with Beedens of Northampton. It was discovered derelict in the 'sixties before restoration in 1970 and is seen at the 1992 Nottingham rally of the AEC Society. Its driver, Bryan Gibson, has brought it to virtually all the society's events. It has the Tylor four-cylinder engine standard for the type. Jack Henley, the owner also has a 1944 ex-Army Matador, still used as a recovery vehicle for his transport business. (A. Townsin)

Despite AEC's removal from Walthamstow to Southall, completed by circa 1927, this disc from a key ring inscribed "A.E.Co. WORKS. WALTHAMSTOW, DEPT – SAFE ROOM" was found by Brian Goulding in the former works premises when visiting the site on 20th October 1984. (P. Rowlett)

The 1954 'airing' of old London buses to mark the Omnibus Society's 25th anniversary aroused considerable public interest and may well have helped to trigger more general interest in the preservation of historic commercial vehicles which began to gain momentum about four years later. Here S742, with B340 alongside and K424 bringing up the rear, are seen parked behind the Earls Court exhibition building in the area usually reserved for demonstrators, before setting off on the run through central London to Waterloo Place, Pall Mall. Inside, the Commercial Motor Show display included brand new RM1, on the AEC stand. At that period, London Transport's collection of old vehicles, which had been stored in various garages over the years, very rarely appeared in public and the idea of a London Transport Museum was yet to come.   (A. Townsin collection)

Reversing into place at Earls Court on the same occasion is NS1995. The NS type represented a major advance on the previous high-floor K and S types. The type was introduced in 1923, its lower build, achieved by the use of a drop rear axle which, in essence, incorporated the drop-centre principle used much later on Bristol Lodekka, Daimler Fleetline and other buses. It was intended from the start to have a covered top deck, but the Metropolitan Police did not approve this until January 1926. NS1995 entered service in February 1927 but the pneumatic tyres (first fitted to the type in 1928) and enclosed cab were later modifications – it was among the last to be withdrawn in 1937. Co-author Alan Townsin can remember riding to school in similar buses in Newcastle, also withdrawn that year.   (E. J. Smith)

Creditable though London Transport's responsible view towards historic vehicles has been, Barry Weatherhead's restoration of K502 is a remarkable achievement. The K type, introduced in 1919, has its place in history because of its half-cab forward-control layout, then new and to remain characteristic of many new buses in Britain for half a century. This particular vehicle was delivered to the LGOC's Plumstead Garage in December 1920, working mainly on the 53 route between West Hampstead and Plumstead Common, though later transferred to Old Kent Road. When withdrawn in 1931 it was sold together with about 500 others to the Cockayne Hartley Egg Packing for use as a henhouse but was purchased around 1939 by a farmer at Orwell, Cambridgeshire, for use as a living van, being occupied as such until the early 'sixties. Barry acquired it for restoration in 1968, the process taking ten years, many parts having to be made from original drawings. He also has a 1906 MOC which he plans to restore, it being one of the vehicles built by the Vanguard concern at Walthamstow and thus in some senses a predecessor to later LGOC and AEC vehicles, though built from parts supplied by Armstrong Whitworth of Newcastle.   (B. Goulding)

Although surviving AEC vehicles from the 1930s are relatively numerous – possibly more so in proportion to output than those of any comparable maker – Miss Muriel Morley's 1931 Regal can truly be described as unique among examples of that period in its combination of being owned by her family and its firm (founded by her father, J. O. Morley) from new and having coach bodywork in virtually original condition. Provincial Garage (Leicester) Ltd continued to run a largely AEC fleet – which, remarkably even at that date, still included JF 2378 among its active members, until 1966. This vehicle is an excellent example of the Regal 662-type chassis in early form, retaining Marles steering, for example, rather than the worm and nut type which became general the following year. The Burlingham bodywork is to a design which was quite popular choice for Regal chassis among independent operators at the time, understandably so as its proportions seemed to suit the chassis particularly well in the idiom of that period, with quite low build. It is good to learn that the six-cylinder 110mm-bore petrol engine has recently been overhauled by Harry Pick, who knows a thing or two about making AEC engines perform correctly, quite apart from being President and Chairman of the AEC Society – this view shows it at its 1988 rally.   (B. Goulding)

6-type survivors

The AEC Society has tended to be lucky with weather for its annual rally, but the first, in 1984, was an exception. Even so, this view of two of the vehicles of the Tideswell family, of Kingsley, near Stoke-on-Trent, almost recreates a workaday scene from an earlier era when such vehicles worked day in day out in all weathers. In front is JJ 9221, its registration a London mark dating from 1933, representing the six-cylinder Mammoth goods models of that era (this one with 8.8-litre oil engine) and behind is a Mammoth Major Mark II eight-wheeler of 1936.   (B. Goulding)

One of the most important finds among AEC vehicles whose survival was previously unknown in recent years is this Regal, originally placed in service 60 years ago by Orange Brothers of Bedlington, Northumberland, and used to inaugurate a London-Newcastle-Edinburgh-Glasgow express service. It was one of four Regals dating from June 1932, two including this vehicle, TY 9608, with Strachans bodywork, though the other two by Weymann were quite similar. They were reputed to be quite high-geared and capable of 60 mph. The major part of the Orange Bros concern was taken over by the Tilling and British Automobile Traction group in 1934 and continued as a separate business running London-Newcastle express services, though put under the management of United Automobile Services Ltd, and effectively becoming part of that concern. This vehicle, like others of its generation, was later transferred to United's own ownership and downgraded to bus work, probably about 1938. At one time it was thought a body exchange with another vehicle had occurred – Alan Townsin confesses to being the probable source of this erroneous report, evidently due to confusion with other instances among United Regals transferred from coach duties – but the body was modified in various detail respects including the fitting of a larger destination display, similar to those of new United ECW-bodied buses of 1939-40. He recalls seeing it in service frequently on local Northumberland area routes into Newcastle up to 1947 or so and it evidently continued thus until being withdrawn in 1950, latterly being allocated to Berwick depot, whose destination blind was still in place when discovered. It was bought as temporary accommodation by a family near Ripon while a house was built, but was then retained for holiday letting, a roof being built over it. The late Mike Heard discovered it some years ago and the owners were eventually persuaded to part with it in 1991 by Ian Hunter of Leeds and fellow United enthusiast Bob Kell. It proved to be basically sound and complete apart from seats and minor fittings. The engine retains its Claudel Hobson carburettor and Bosch electrics – it turned over fairly easily after 40 years of inactivity and was subsequently started up. Although mostly painted dark green, part of the United red paint survived on the nearside, including part of the fleetname. The vehicle has since been sold to the chief engineer of the Caldaire group of companies, nowadays owners of the United concern, and a full restoration is soon to begin.   (Leo Pratt)

The lower photograph shows TY 9608 when in service as United AR15 at Haymarket, Newcastle, in 1946/7. The body had been rebuilt, almost certainly by United at its Darlington works in a manner not uncommon at the time, with bus seats (probably from some other vehicle), sliding-vent opening windows and continuous metal louvre over them. It was intended to make the vehicle sound and serviceable for a few more years rather than in any sense a restoration, yet the quality of work was quite high, as usual with United.

(R. A. Mills, Roy Marshall collection)

In the days when the preserved ex-Tilling ST922 was in regular use in central London on the special route 100 in the 'seventies it was intriguing to find how it simply went about its business with a complete absence of drama, keeping up with modern traffic without difficulty despite having first entered service about half a century earlier. It was new to Thos. Tilling Ltd in November 1930, passing to the newly-formed London Transport in 1933 and ceasing passenger service in December 1946 though it is noteworthy that, like many of the type, it spent much of the war period on loan to a provincial operator, in this case Midland Red in 1941-44. It was one of those converted to mobile canteen duty, running in this form from 1947 to 1954, later passing to a dealer and owing its survival to purchase by the late Prince Marshall in 1966 – it was restored and re-entered service with Obsolete Fleet in 1972, being seen here in Piccadilly ten years later. From this view the Tilling design of open-stair body standard for these buses appears to belong to an earlier era than the Regent chassis.   (B. Goulding)

Generally speaking, London Transport has not favoured the preservation of the first vehicles of the various types that have been run over the years, doubtless arguing that they were apt to be unrepresentative. An exception is trolleybus number 1, numerically the first of the pioneer fleet of 60 AEC 663T vehicles placed in service by London United Tramways Ltd in 1931, which was selected to be kept when withdrawn in 1949. There had been earlier experiments, but LUT, part of the Underground group, introduced regular trolleybus operation to London with four local routes based on Fulwell depot. The vehicles were a curious mixture of ideas, for the chassis, which had their motors at the front under a bonnet, and the general layout of the bodies, resembled the LGOC's contemporary LT-class motor buses, but the appearance of the bodywork had a strong affinity to the LUT's contemporary Feltham trams, both being built by the Union Construction Co, also an associated concern. Number 1, which had been in the Clapham Museum, was brought back for the final day of London trolleybus operation, again based on Fulwell, on 8th May 1962 and its next time in passenger-carrying service was at the Carlton Colville Museum in July 1990, as seen here in company with number 1858, an HR/2 tram also from the London Transport (in this case originally London County Council) fleet. The East Anglia Transport Museum collection also houses BUT trolleybuses from the Newcastle and Ashton municipal fleets and Brighton Hove & District as well as an ex-Nottingham AEC Regent tower-wagon of particular interest because it is converted to normal control, all being owned by the London Trolleybus Preservation Society. (B. Goulding)

There are many preserved AEC vehicles that can be described as important from a historical point of view, but there can be no doubt of the justification in this case. The rigid eight-wheeled goods vehicle has been such a familiar sight for over half a century in Britain but it was AEC that first introduced it in internal-combustion form – there had been some Sentinel steamers but the era of steam was already coming to a close. The original 680-type Mammoth Major eight-wheeler went into production in June 1934, and although some research by Gordon Baron (see AEC Society Gazette No. 17) has shown that the vehicle nowadays owned by the Science Museum, 680014 was built in September of that year, and thus not quite as early as had been thought, being one of two for J. M. Mills Ltd of Liverpool to transport industrial alcohol, it is believed to be the only survivor of the 680 type. A total of 34 were built, including two 'official' conversions from 668-type six-wheelers, and all but three had 8.8-litre oil engines, generally A165K type with Ricardo-head as built, but the Mills vehicles were among three exceptions, having A162A petrol engines of the 110mm-bore high-power head type. Normal production of the 680 type ended in 1935 (though the final vehicle, a conversion, was produced at an unspecified later date and had an A180J toroidal 8.8 unit). It is seen at the rally to celebrate 60 years of the AEC Regent held at the Science Museum's premises at Wroughton in 1989 – the AEC six-cylinder petrol engine and D124 gearbox sound was pleasantly familiar but it seemed incongruous coming from an eight-wheeler. The excellent restoration was supervised by Harry Pick.

The Science Museum's collection includes several other AEC, including a Q chassis, a 1931 Regal single-deck bus originally of Red Bus Service, Mansfield) and London RM and RF type vehicles. (A. Townsin)

Representative of the lighter AEC goods models of the early 'thirties is this 1934 Monarch tipper, used by Bracebridge Mental Hospital, Lincoln, and preserved by Colin Garton of the Lincoln Vintage Vehicle Society. (L.V.V.S.)

Q-type coaches were never a common sight and when this photograph was taken on 1st June 1957 in Nottingham it is unlikely that any other example could still be found on excursion duty. It had been new to its owners, J. H. Woolliscroft & Son, of Darley Dale, Derbyshire, using the fleetname Silver Service just 27 years earlier, and was the only example of its type with Willowbrook body, built to a high-floor design which permitted forward-facing seating for all 37 passengers. Usually a longitudinal seat was placed over the engine – still the original petrol unit – the grilles for which are evident rearwards of the front offside wheel. Originally there had been no front grille, but otherwise it was little altered from new. Also visible is a Willowbrook-bodied Regal IV of the same owners. When the Q was withdrawn it was bought for preservation but its future was uncertain for a time. Tony Peart, well-known for his preserved Regent III buses, stepped in to save it but in 1981 it passed to the British Commercial Vehicle Museum at Leyland where it is in store – the body requires much work and restoration will be a costly if very desirable project. (R. Marshall)

The successor to the 680-type Mammoth Major eight-wheeler was the Mark II version of the model, 0386, reduced in weight to meet new legislation. The 7.7-litre engine was adopted as standard, together with extensive use of light alloys, making it possible to bring the unladen weight below 6 tons with a suitably light body and cab and thus carry 16 tons within the then 22 ton gross limit. Among the customers was the Bath & Portland Stone Firms Ltd where number 1 (CLJ 995), seen here, was delivered in December 1936 – it was chassis number 0386170, indicating increased sales as compared to the previous heavier model – six more were bought by this fleet over the next two years. Its regular driver in early post war days delivering limestone, mainly to London and Gravesend, was Stan Hawkins and though he left the area for his native South Wales, his son Dave, who'd ridden with his father as a boy, kept in touch and asked the firm if he could save CLJ – eventually this happened in 1969 though the vehicle was still in road use until 1964. Stan tackled the restoration as a retirement job though Dave, who has a large collection of AECs, took over in 1984 when his father was ill. It is seen in Scammell's works at the 1987 AEC Society rally in Watford. It is still in good order, with a reconditioned 7.7, though top speed is only about 28 mph – the speed limit was 20 mph for such vehicles and low gearing was almost essential with such limited power. (B. Goulding)

Passenger models with 7.7-litre engines were built in large numbers in the later 'thirties for a wide variety of fleets. Reading Corporation standardised on Regent chassis with Park Royal lowbridge bodywork for its bus fleet. Number 47 (RD 7127) belonged to the 1935 batch of three, having chassis number 06613647 – similar buses were delivered yearly up to 1938, having the characteristic Park Royal metal-framed body construction with circular section internal trim on the body pillars. Its restrained maroon and cream livery perhaps makes it self-effacing but Alan Townsin found it capable of quite a lively performance when enjoying a ride in it at the Regent 60th anniversary gathering at Wroughton in 1989, where he took this photograph. It is owned by J. Whitehead of Reading., as custodian for the Trolleybus Preservation Society.

The London Transport 9T9 batch of Green Line coaches of 1936 represented an attempt to give a 'modernised' appearance, perhaps influenced by a perceived need for something different to keep up the undertaking's reputation for up-to-date design in view of the almost contemporary batch of Green Line Q-type coaches. The built-up wing gave a hint of later ideas but the bonnet raised above the radiator gave a rather unsatisfactory effect not repeated. Weymann built the body to LT specification. The 7.7-litre engined vehicles were rather overshadowed by the 10T10 type of similar body design but more orthodox front appearance on 8.8-litre chassis of 1938. Seen here at Weybridge station on the Cobham Bus Museum special service in 1984 is T448, saved for preservation by the late Alan Allmey but on his death taken over by his brother Donald, though later passed to the London Bus Preservation Group of Cobham. (B. Goulding)

Leeds City Transport took to the 7.7-litre Regent with preselective transmission with great enthusiasm, basing its fleet intake almost entirely on the type from 1934 to the period between December 1939 and March 1940, when the final batch of 20 were delivered. Somehow its examples seemed to run more smoothly than most of the type. Almost all the vehicles from December 1936 onwards had the bow-fronted style of Roe bodywork, but only the final HUM-registered batch had the curved outline windscreen and sliding-vent windows shown. Number 106 was retained for non-passenger duties and lay dumped behind one of LCT's depots, passing with the undertaking to West Yorkshire PTE until Geoffrey Hilditch, then Director of Engineering, decided it should be restored to original condition with the distinctive blue livery, though strictly speaking it should have the deeper radiator standard from 1937 and a conventional filler cap. It is seen at the Leyland 90th anniversary gathering in 1986. (B. Goulding)

Some preserved vehicles take on a special kind of individual fame, often because of their history. Number 35 (BOR 767) of the Gosport & Fareham Omnibus Co (Provincial) fleet, one of the original 1936 batch of four similar vehicles on Regent 7.7-litre chassis with Park Royal bodywork which constituted the first delivery of new double-deck buses to that operator, had achieved a degree of fame when withdrawn in 1967, for it is believed to have been the oldest double-deck bus with original bodywork in regular service in Britain. Even so, it was in generally very sound condition, aided by the teak body framing specified for these vehicles. David Whitaker's father worked for the company and David had spent every free moment round the fleet, so when his father phoned to say that BOR 767 was for sale, there could only be one response. It is still in remarkably original order, as seen in this view with a contemporary Austin 10, though strictly speaking, the radiator is of the post-1937 type – maybe a swap should be made with the Leeds bus on the previous page! David also has an ex-Provincial Regal 4, albeit with 7.7-litre six-cylinder engine and much rebuilt body, as running in later years. (J. Quartly)

Co-author Alan Townsin confesses to a rather special affection for FUF 63, the Regent first registered on 31st March 1939 for operation by Brighton Corporation and purchased soon after withdrawal in 1965 by Mike Dryhurst for preservation – he is at the wheel in this view at the 1987 AEC Society rally in Watford. Alan recalls the pleasure of driving it across London and for parts of the journey to and from Halifax for a rally in 1968, and still rates it one of the most enjoyable buses to drive, old or new, he has ever tried, with beautifully responsive controls. Brighton chose a mechanical specification not unlike the 10T10 Green Line coaches for these vehicles, with pot-cavity 8.8-litre engines and preselective gearboxes, though with much lower-geared rear axles to suit Brighton's hills – there was a certain glee in overtaking a Leyland Atlantean, then almost new, on an uphill climb in Sheffield, though motorway driving at no more than 34 mph was not such fun and surprisingly noisy in the cab – the passengers get a much quieter ride. The lines of the Weymann metal-framed body seemed almost perfectly suited to the chassis and the red and cream livery then common to both Corporation and Brighton Hove & District company buses. (B. Goulding)

A whole new era in bus design, not merely for London Transport or AEC, began with the appearance of RT1 in 1938. Strictly speaking, the preserved vehicle bearing that number and the correct registration EYK 396 does not have the chassis of the original RT1, being that of RT1420, a 1949 vehicle at first having a Cravens body which was damaged beyond repair in 1955 when driven under a low bridge. The chassis of RT1 was dismantled in 1946 but the original body survived, being transferred to RT19 and then in 1956 mounted on the chassis from RT1420 to form a mobile training vehicle bearing the number 1037J in the service fleet and operated on trade plates. It was this that was restored by the late Prince Marshall and given the original registration number, being seen here together with RT133, one of the first production batch, restored to original 1940 condition in this photograph taken at the London Transport 50th anniversary celebrations at Chiswick in 1983. (B. Goulding)

Military interlude

Surviving examples of the Matador 0853 mainly built in the 1939-45 war period and closely related types are numerous. Many are modern-day equivalents of the biblical exhortation to turn swords into ploughshares, being converted from military to such civilian uses as recovery vehicles or timber tractors. Quite a number are still in use, though others have been restored to original condition, like the example nearest the camera in this imposing line-up at the 1991 AEC Society rally in Nottingham. Its cab is of the type with 'ventilated' roof skin developed as an attempt to counter heat build-up on vehicles operating in North Africa. (B. Goulding)

At the beginning of the war, the emphasis was largely on the Marshal model 644, a design dating back to 1931 and conforming to an Army specification for a 6 x 4 chassis with four-cylinder petrol engine but based on mainly standard 6-type units; other makers produced directly comparable models. This photograph of one out on pre-delivery test was sent by Dick Cuff, seen at the wheel and still going strong at the age of 87 – the date is thought to have been soon after the war began in September 1939.

The basis of the main military models built in the 1939-45 period was a series of all-wheel-drive chassis developed by Hardy Motors Ltd, originally of Slough, but which transferred to Southall in 1932 and was described as 'allied to' AEC before being completely absorbed in 1938. Among early productions was this example quoted as type R6/8, built in 1932 for the Iraq Petroleum Co Ltd to carry sections of 12in. dia pipe in 15-ton loads for pipelines then being built to link Kirkuk with Tripoli and Haifa, the latter then in Palestine – Iraq was then under British mandate. The chassis had a standard 120 bhp 110-bore petrol engine, two gearboxes giving six speeds and worm drive for all three axles. The trailer was made by Eagle. This AEC official photograph of the vehicle with a test load was taken at Southall works and is also of interest by virtue of the two Green Line coaches on Regal chassis, just visible on the left, one identifiable as T256 of the 1931 batch and the other a rear-entrance 1930 vehicle carrying a route board for service Q, which operated to Uxbridge at that time, using the AEC works as a garage, probably mainly for wage-rate reasons, though three very early oil-engined T-class coaches were used on the route.

A rare legacy from the Hardy era is this vehicle, an R6/T, the military-style 6 x 6 model which was given the AEC model number 850 and of which some 33 were built between 1932 and 1936 – a leaflet issued in 1933 shows four examples described as a "fifth repeat order for H.M. War Dept.". This model had a broad radiator, the outline of which can be seen on the dash panel; its top tank had a rounded profile unsuited to the triangle badge which was therefore attached to the dash as shown. All three axles had large hub covers, presumably containing epicyclic reduction gears and part of the robust front suspension designed to allow negotiation of rough ground can be seen. The vehicle shown is owned by Derek Lambe, the photo taken at a location near Peterborough by Brian Goulding in April 1984. The series of model numbers thus begun was linked to some of AEC's most famous projects – 851 is quoted in a list compiled by the technical sales department in 1965 as "8-wheel tractor", presumably the Road Train type illustrated on a later page of this book, of which four are quoted in the 1933 to 1935 period; 852 was allocated to the pre-war railcars, also a Hardy venture originally, with 38 produced between 1933 and 1940, and then came the 853 and O853 beginning in 1939, to which the Matador name already in use for civilian models was extended, destined to be the most familiar of all.

The Hardy-derived designs moved into the big time with the O853 put into production in 1939, just in time for the war. They were each given thorough testing on rough ground, with a box containing a test load, temporary rear mudguards and very basic-looking bits of tin to act as windscreens. Dick Cuff is at the wheel, with Terry Donovan and Sam Mooney in this scene about 1943. Dick also tested AEC armoured cars, of which every 25th vehicle went to Farnborough, fully loaded with dummy ammunition and other weights, to confirm its ability to climb and restart in either direction on a 1 in 2½ radient. (D. Cuff)

Who could have guessed that working Matador O853 models would still be quite a common sight half a century or so later? These three, still in fairground service with the Harris family were seen at the Ardingly vintage show and rally, July 1990. Only one of the three still had the 7.7-litre engine, two having received AV470 units, which became quite a popular replacement as parts for the 7.7 became difficult to obtain. (Graham Edge)

The advent of four-engined Stirling and Halifax bombers in the Royal Air Force in early 1941. created a need for much larger capacity tankers, capable of working over soft ground. The Air Ministry turned to AEC and the 854 was the result – broadly speaking, a 6 x 6 equivalent to the Matador O853, on which could be built a 2,500-gallon tanker with pump for rapid refuelling of bombers. The choice of the petrol engine appears to have been quite deliberate – the O853 used the 7.7-litre oil engine in A187 form (based on the civilian direct-injection A173) which had been introduced for it in April 1939, and certainly a vehicle for the RAF would have had high priority at that date – but, for the 854 (and also the 853 petrol version of the Matador), the A193 engine was introduced in May 1940, based on the A162 'high power head' 110mm-bore 7.4-litre engine that had been standard for AEC's six-cylinder petrol models since 1932, differing from it notably in sump shape to clear the driven front axle. The use of semi-floating rear axles was doubtless because AEC had not at that stage developed fully-floating units suitable for the cross-country bogie (there had been a similar though shorter time-lag in the switch of passenger bogie, not triggered until London's big demand for six-wheel trolleybuses from 1935). Production of the 854 began in August 1940 and 463 chassis were built in the period up to July 1942. By then the switch to 7.7 oil-engine power had been accepted and production of the 0854, with A196 engine (based on the A187 and A173) began in May 1942, continuing until 1947, latterly with a new fully-floating rear bogie, during which period 1,431 chassis were built. This photograph taken at Mepal, Cambridgeshire, shows a Lancaster of 75 Squadron being refuelled by 'Dumbo', one of these refuellers – the Lanc. could carry 2,154 gallons, nearly emptying the tanker, if low, a task that would take about 50 minutes. The wide radiator fitted to some examples may have been needed to avoid the petrol engine overheating during this process.   (H. H. Stratford)

A striking parallel to the above scene from half a century later. Here what was thought to be the last AEC in Gulf War colours is seen in February 1992 at Markham, Norfolk, parked alongside another veteran of that conflict, a Victor XH672 – itself a tanker – bearing emblems recording 52 air-to-air refuelling sorties. The RAF is thought now to be the third largest user of AEC vehicles, after Rodoviaria Nacional of Portugal and London Transport, with about 150 of these Mammoth Major refuellers still in use. This example, dating from about 1973, still had some red desert sand in the cab.   (B. Goulding)

Two Matadors owned by friends and based at Glan Conwy, a little south of Llandudno, are still liable to be called out – often together – to rescue stranded vehicles or machinery. For example, in 1989 the Llandudno lifeboat Caterpillar tractor was submerged by the tide after becoming stuck in the sand, as did a Moxy 6 x 6 dumper sent to rescue it. Tom Buckley's Matador UFX 366 (chassis number O8531888) pulled the dumper out, and is seen below climbing the promenade steps after this phase of the operation. Tom does regular lifting work for the RNLI, for which they receive no bills. The following morning he was joined by Harry Lightfoot with his vehicle and the two winched the Cat free in seconds. The other Matador at Glan Conwy is Harry Lightfoot's WFX 274 (08536495) which has a replacement cab. It is seen (below right) winching a Priestman digger out of the river Conway – Tom's vehicle was also present on this occasion, just out of the picture on the right, hauling another cable.   (Tom Yates, RNLI; H. Lightfoot)

This 1943 Coles crane on O854 chassis is representative of 192 vehicles built on both petrol and oil-engined versions of the models for use by the RAF – the crane has a Ford V8 petrol engine and a safe working load of 5 tons. Survivors of the 854 and O854 models in civilian use into later years were much less common than of the O853 Matador, though some of the crane version found such applications – Alan Townsin recalls a petrol example converted to a concrete breaker in use when the AEC drawing office building at Southall works was extended in about 1953. This one, looking much as it did when new, was photographed in recent times at High Ercall, a former RAF airfield in Shropshire where such vehicles had been used. (Graham Lycett)

The intermediate post-war passenger models belong to a period from which relatively few vehicles have survived, being rather overshadowed by the slightly later Mark III era. Some did find new and relatively glamorous roles however – this commercial postcard from Victoria, British Columbia, on the west coast of Canada, shows what are claimed to be "Double-decker London buses", and while Leyland RTL579 at the rear was genuine enough, the leading vehicle is ACH 646, a Regent II which probably never saw London again after it left Southall as a chassis bound for the Willowbrook works at Loughborough for bodying and thence to join the fleet of Trent Motor Traction Co Ltd in 1948, operating in Derbyshire or nearby – even so, it reinforced Victoria's reputation of fondness for Anglophile tastes. It is now in a local museum. (B. Goulding collection)

During the latter part of the war, from about 1943, though production of civilian chassis was generally at a standstill, AEC supplied 7.7-litre oil engines to Bristol, Daimler, ERF and Maudslay, and this continued for some time in the early post-war years. Those supplied to Daimler during the war period went into CWA6 chassis, a model generally regarded as an unfamiliar hybrid. Coventry City Transport, however, had used AEC engines in pre-war chassis, of type COA6, and in the early post-war years standardised on the CVA6 model, still using the 7.7-litre unit. This example, number 94 (GKV 94) dating from 1950, was preserved and attended the 1992 AEC Society rally in Nottingham – it has been owned by Messrs Holloway, Crossey and Bunker of Rugby since 1971. (A. A. Townsin)

Still earning its keep is HKL 826, a Regal I model originally placed in service with Maidstone & District Motor Services Ltd in September 1946 and which had its original Beadle bus body cut down to open-topped form originally for use on Hastings town tour duties, passing to Hastings & District on its foundation, but in more recent times acquired by Guide Friday, with whom it was seen on a Cotswold tour in May 1991. The front mudguards had been refashioned by M&D to give a Mark III-style look. (W. J. N. Barlow)

Mark III – a golden age

Preserved RT-type buses from the huge post-war deliveries made to London Transport between 1947 and 1954 are numerous, many of them faithful restorations of these splendid vehicles in their younger days. In one sense they represent a triumph of standardisation, mostly having bodywork made to identical design by Park Royal and Weymann, yet over the period of production and subsequent overhauls variety crept in, even if only in minor elements. Representing typical red and green variants at the 1991 AEC Society rally are RT981 (JXN 9), originally delivered as a country area (green) bus with 'top box' Weymann-built RT3-type body in 1948 but with later Park Royal-built body in central area red livery as seen here, and, on the left of the picture, RT4494 (OLD 714). The latter was one of a batch of chassis which received overhauled Park Royal bodies which had originally been on the SRT-class rebuilds from STL chassis and, on transfer to new RT chassis, repainted green for Green Line duty, entering service in this form in 1954. This vehicle later passed to London Country but was restored to original style after withdrawal in 1972. RT 981 is owned by P. Hockley of Odsal, Bradford and RT 4494 by D. Gray of Lincoln. (A. A. Townsin)

The emphasis on exports led AEC to produce its mirror-image left-hand models, the effect being conveyed in this scene at the Leyland 90th anniversary rally held at Leyland in July 1986. On the left, a 9631E model, with not merely appearance but the whole chassis, including 9.6-litre engine and preselective gearbox and cab layout, to suit its left-hand steering, placed in service in 1950 with Carris of Lisbon and then recently returned to Britain into the ownership of the British Commercial Vehicle Museum. On the right, a right-hand Regal III, in this case a 6821A model with 7.7-litre engine and crash gearbox having Windover coach bodywork that had been operated by Trent Motor Traction Co Ltd. (B. Goulding)

The degree of commitment liable to be needed for preservation of an old vehicle is conveyed by this picture taken just over two years later of the ex-Trent Regal III seen in the photograph above, with body stripped to the frame and extensive re-timbering in progress, the opportunity being taken to remove most chassis units and carry out such restoration as proved necessary. The vehicle had been acquired by Burton's Coach Hire, of Alfreton, in September 1987 and had reached the stage shown a year later. The view reveals the characteristic flowing curves of the Mark III passenger frame, designed to make the most effective use of the materials and give strength without excessive weight, yet elegant in themselves even though not visible once the body was completed – like most intended as coaches, it has the drop rear extension of the side-members, very like a double-decker, but in this case to suit the rear luggage boot incorporated in the body. (John Burton)

Another story of perseverance – three stages in the life of a Regent III 9613A model, KDT 393, placed in service by Doncaster Corporation as its number 22, complete with Roe bodywork, in 1951. In the top left view it is seen still in virtually new condition in September 1953, at the Leicester Avenue terminus, with no more than a build-up of dirt around the rear hub, evidently due to a defective grease seal. In the 'sixties it passed to a local independent operator, Blue Ensign, still looking quite smart in a pale blue livery, and then to Basford Driving School, Nottingham, but the deterioration evident in the view above in the late 'seventies followed several years of inactivity at Sandtoft. However, D. A. (Tony) Peart, whose home is in Doncaster, took it in hand and the 1988 view at the Sandwell rally, left, shows it restored to as-new appearance, reminding onlookers how effective a traditional-style maroon livery relieved by three cream bands can look. Tony thus has two Regent III Roe buses, but the York Pullman example which was his first acquistion differs in being one of the rare 6812A type with 7.7-litre engine. A feature in common between both of these and also the coach shown below is the use of the crash gearbox as signified by the A suffix to the type number. (D. A. Peart)

Some restored vehicles still earn their keep. Alan Townsin has a sentimental attachment for the fleet of Regal III 9621A models with Duple bodywork that Devon General placed in service with its Grey Cars excursion fleet in 1948 and 1950, for when on honeymoon in Torquay in 1951 he and his late wife went on a trip to Buckfast Abbey in one. He confesses he didn't take note of which one, but it could well have been LTA 629, seen here still on touring duties with Classique Sun Saloon Luxury Coaches of Paisley at Tarbert, Isle of Harris in the Outer Hebrides in June 1991 – it is good to think that there may be young couples following suit 40 years later. It is this vehicle that is portrayed in original livery in the recent Corgi model – it is understandable that the body design is the FS1 variant, with one more side window, for that was the more common variant than the FS13 peculiar to the Regal III and Corgi can use the moulding for several chassis makes if it so wishes, but it is a pity that more care was not taken to reproduce the AEC radiator's subtle curves, seen here very clearly, for the Corgi interpretation is much too angular. (W. S. N. Barlow)

Although Brian Goulding's activities as founder of the AEC Society and immense enthusiasm for all things related to AEC, not least the collection of a huge amount of material for this book, are well known, the fact that he owned a Regent III for a time is not so well known, writes Alan Townsin. In October 1973, Huddersfield Corporation was selling off some 9613E models dating from 1955. They were among the last built despite having chassis numbers which might have been thought appropriate to a 1950 bus, for they had been allocated a batch of numbers left blank by part of an order for Nottingham that had been delayed at the operator's request and then cancelled in favour of Mark V chassis. He put in a bid for £225, becoming the proud owner of 9613E4925, Huddersfield 243 (JVH 373), including tyres, batteries and a full tank of fuel. It had covered 451,814 miles on Huddersfield's hilly routes when withdrawn in July 1973, but proved fully reliable. The batch of ten had East Lancashire bodywork, this being one of four with 58-seat capacity, 30 on top and 28 below, a high figure for a lowbridge 27ft. bus. It is seen in company with Eastbourne 42 (then owned by Eastbourne Regent Preservation Group but later purchased by Gerald Truran), a 1951 bus on chassis

9613A5636 and having highbridge bodywork of similar design but built by East Lancs associate concern, Bruce Coachworks of Cardiff at a rally held by the St. Helens Trolleybus and Transport Society in March 1974, the first

event JVH 373 attended after purchase. Brian's work took him to California, causing him to sell it in 1977, and it passed via David Heap to its current owner Glyn Sykes. It is good to be able to record its reappeance after a 15-year layoff at the May 1992 Heart of the Pennines Rally.   (B. Goulding)

Rather surprisingly, AEC did not get involved with fire engines to any appreciable extent until the post-war period when Merryweather began to use the Regent III chassis, sometimes almost in standard form, though usually shortened, but in other cases considerably modified. This example, new to Kent Fire Brigade with 100ft. escape, has the standard radiator projecting further forward than usual – the registration suggests it dates from 1957. It is preserved and is seen here at Duxford in May 1989.   (Peter Rowlett)

A bonneted design was also produced, still with Regent III chassis design but in some cases at least having a Meadows 10-litre petrol engine with two carburettors and carrying a quite different radiator, doubtless designed to be distinctive though having a slight echo of some pre-war Crossley designs. This one evidently dating from c.1950 had been operated by Kingston on Hull Fire Brigade and, latterly at least, has a Leyland 400 engine. It is seen in August 1987 after acquisition by Ron Fox, proprietor of Fox Coaches, Towcester, being seen here at Crich. A somewhat similar vehicle with the Meadows engine, but with 'saloon' body, was built for Birkenhead Fire Brigade in 1952 and has recently been acquired by E. J. Billingham of Morden, Surrey – it had been involved in an accident and the fire brigade workshops had produced a squared-up replacement for the grille.   (B. Goulding)

Understandably the winner of many awards is Richard Cresswell's Mammoth Major Mark III six-wheeler, which encapsulates the look of a typical AEC goods vehicle of that era, with 9.6-litre engine and the elegantly-proportioned standard design of cab, built by various concerns in accordance with AEC's drawings. The Fordson tractor carried is of the type once not only the most familiar on farms all over Britain but was also used by AEC itself to shunt chassis around the Southall works until they reached a stage when they could be driven under their own power. The Mammoth Major dates from 1951 and was built for the War Office though operated by the Air Ministry, later passing to a contractor from whom it was bought for preservation by Richard Creswell in 1976 – the livery of green with red relief and style of lettering seems to suit it perfectly. It is seen at the 1992 AEC Society rally at Nottingham. Richard also has a 1958 Mercury with Cravens Homalloy cab and a 1961 twin-steering Mustang, all three kept in immaculate order. (A. A. Townsin)

The Air Ministry continued its choice of AEC chassis for aircraft refuelling duties following the precedent set by the 854 and O854 in wartime. Vehicles for use on airfields with concrete surfaces for aircraft parking areas did not need all-wheel-drive and so the standard Mammoth Major Mark III six-wheeler was chosen, though the refuelling equipment began to be more sophisticated, with long booms to facilitate rapid replenishment of aircraft fuel tanks. Similar vehicles are still to be found on numerous civil airfields today, as well as providing a basis for restoration in several cases, usually with platform bodywork. This scene shows one with F86 Sabre jet fighter. (Air Ministry)

There had been a lull in manufacture of vehicles for military duty after the 1939-45 war, but in the early 'fifties fresh orders were placed, partly due to the outbreak of the Korean war and some general unease about the possibility of more conflicts. Specifications for a new generation of military vehicle were issued to interested manufacturers and AEC's response was the O859 6 x 4 and O860 6 x 6 models, using the 11.3-litre engine and given the name Militant. Officially, these were 'interim' designs, for the War Department had rather grandiose ideas of a more elaborately standardised range, but in practice these models were to give excellent service. Even so, it is unlikely that anyone could have foreseen that over 30 years after their introduction some would be operating in the Falkland Islands playing their part in the build-up of defences after the Argentine invasion had been repulsed. An O860 is seen near Port Stanley in February 1985. (B. Goulding)

The new mediumweight range introduced in 1953 struck a responsive note, offering a balance of lighter weight than the Mark III range and consequent more nimble performance yet with sufficient of the traditional AEC durability when used intensively to see off most competitors, especially those whose background was from the mass-production end of the market. The oil companies were major users, among them Shell Mex and BP Ltd, the joint marketing organisation that fed both Shell and BP filling stations. This Mercury with AV470 engine, now owned by Shell UK Ltd, dates from 1958 and is noteworthy historically in having the first tank to carry petroleum spirit to have been made from aluminium, built by Hawker Siddeley and carrying 1,000 gallons in four compartments. It was extensively tested at the MIRA proving ground before entering normal service from Hamble depot for 10 years. The cab is generally typical of Mercury models of that period, though the horizontally divided opening driver's windscreen was a traditional feature becoming rare by that date, evidently specified by the operator. It is seen at the 1991 Nottingham rally. (A. A. Townsin)

Mediumweights

Using basically similar major units, the Reliance passenger chassis was equally successful, often attracting orders from fleets not hitherto AEC users. That did not apply to Scottish Omnibuses Ltd, which inherited general favour towards AEC chassis for a major part of its fleet requirements from its predecessor Scottish Motor Traction Co Ltd (whose monogram continued to be displayed) extending back as far as the early 'thirties. The SMT monogram was still carried on this 1959 Reliance 2MU3RV, one of a batch of 20 with Alexander 38-seat bodywork having glass cantrail windows for touring and similar duties. It was purchased for preservation after withdrawal in 1975, originally in Northern Ireland, but later with the Scottish Bus Museum – it is seen at the Fleetwood tram Sunday event in July 1991. (B. Goulding)

An interesting example of a special-purpose vehicle surviving because its capabilities still greatly exceed its replacement cost. It is believed that six of these emergency generating sets were built at a cost of £22,500 each in 1965, based on a Mercury GM4RA chassis and having a Centrax gas turbine to drive a 400Kw generator – replacement at today's prices would be £250,000. This example, with registration DTA 983C which suggests a Devon origin, still serves with Norweb at its Bolton depot, Another is with British Gas at Nuneaton, one is believed to be in the Middle East, and the sister vehicle to the one shown, which was also based at Bolton, was cut up in 1977, leaving the fate of two unknown. The typical Mercury cab design had graduated to the curved windscreen form by the 'sixties. (Norweb)

Claimed to be the oldest Reliance still in regular use is KHJ 999, a 1955 example with Harrington Wayfarer bodywork operated by Clive Screaton's Grand Edwardian Touring Company of Norcott Brook, near Warrington. It is seen, left, during a coffee break at Rest and Be Thankful, during a Scottish tour in May 1990 – note the slogan 'powered by AEC – possibly Britain's finest PSV chassis'. The vehicle was formerly owned by Mulley's Motorways, itself a fleet with many long-serving AEC vehicles. The principle on which the tours – all run by five Reliance coaches of the 1955-73 period – are operated is unhurried relaxation, as conveyed by the scene within KHJ 999 as afternoon tea is served on a Devon tour – the interior lights switched on for photography give an illusion of darkness outside. Last year the the Continental iteneraries covered included Lapland. (C. Screaton)

When British Railways decided to make a wholesale conversion from steam to diesel power in the 'fifties, a major part of the changeover on the less heavily loaded routes was made by sets of railcars of design derived from the pioneer units built for the Great Western Railway by AEC in the period from 1933-40. Responsibility for this type of work had been transferred to British United Traction from 1946 and thus became a joint AEC and Leyland enterprise. When the bulk orders for British Railways began to come through in the late 'fifties (bringing the phrase 'diesel multiple unit' into the language) the engines used were divided between the two makers, Leyland 680 -powered units often being allocated to northern areas and those with AEC 11.3-litre units more to the midlands and the south. The external appearance, especially that of the cab ends, varied according to builder, the rather 'heavy' looking Metro-Cammell version as built around 1957 being seen here, but the mechanical design apart from the choice of engine was basically of AEC origin. In recent years, a standardisation programme has led to the replacement of AEC engines by Leyland but many have been refurbished for a further period of use. The example shown below is crossing the swing bridge at Reedham over the river Bure on the Norwich-Lowestoft line, in June 1991. (B. Goulding)

A venture which did not live up to expectations was the Monocoach integral single-decker, introduced as a joint venture with Park Royal at the same time as the Reliance in 1953. Its construction, with an underframe built at AEC but so designed that the body pillars could be assembled directly on to the ends of the full-width cross-members, was claimed to give weight-saving benefits. However conventional bodywork built to identical specification on Reliance chassis by Park Royal proved to be only about 2 cwt heavier, so interest in the concept was not maintained after early orders, generally speaking. Booth & Fisher, of Sheffield, had two with lower-than-standard roof line in 1954, and WRA 12, seen here looking a little battered when still in service in 1975, has since been preserved. It is based on chassis MC3RV056. (M. Fowler)

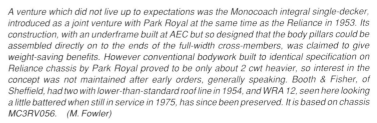

When the Regent V was announced in 1954, the emphasis was on the mediumweight MD3RV version with AV470 engine and several weight-saving features, though the basic chassis design was derived from the Regent III. The grille designed for it was also applied to the Mercury (which began with a plainer version of similar outline) and eventually across all models to which it was suited. Gradually, however, the majority choice among operators swung back to the larger-engined versions, and several operators had not wavered from the view that they could be relied upon to give reliable service. Among them was Ipswich Corporation, which had chosen preselective Regent III and Regal IV models to replace its trolleybuses, and adopted the 9.6-litre version with Monocontrol gearbox for subsequent orders. This example, a 2D2RA model dating from 1963, was purchased from Ipswich for preservation when withdrawn in 1981 but after some years was sold to Carl Ireland of Hull who specialises in conversion of classic buses for trade purposes. Its East Lancs body was converted to open top and the vehicle refurbished for Nichioh Trade Service Co Ltd of Japan, importers of British and French cars, being painted in London Transport-style livery as shown and given the fleet number RM53. It was subsequently sold to a Tokyo operator, being thought to be the first British double-decker to enter passenger service in Japan. (Carl Ireland).

Operators were mixed in their reaction to the new-style bonnet as introduced as standard for the Regent V in response to a trend towards such designs at the time. Nottingham City Transport switched the balance of an outstanding order for 30 vehicles to the new model but specified a combination of features – 9.6-litre engine, synchromesh gearbox and traditional-style radiator – that made the D3RV chassis equivalent to a Regent III 9613S model except for the wider front springs that remained as the minor-seeming but key Mark V feature. Park Royal built the bodywork to its contemporary light-alloy design, producing an attractive overall appearance. A further 35 similar buses were delivered the following year and one of these, Nottingham No. 266, has been restored to original livery and condition. It was purchased for preservation in 1976 and is owned by P. D. Scott of West Bridgford. (B. Goulding)

Halifax Corporation was 'hooked' on the AEC Regent from the very earliest days, taking delivery of three examples in November 1929, adopting its Glasgow-like orange and green livery after an even earlier visit by a demonstrator. For many years the municipal and closely associated joint committee fleets were almost exclusively AEC, and even though Leyland and Daimler secured a share of orders from the post-war period, deliveries of Regent buses continued to the Mark V era. This scene, so typical of the hilly terrain surrounding the town, conveys the atmosphere of bus operation in the area beautifully. However, Regent V LJX 215 (a 2D3RA model with Metro-Cammell body) is not seen soon after entering service as Halifax Joint Omnibus Committee 215 in 1960, as might be thought from the glistening paint and chromium plate, but as preserved by the Mersey & Calder Bus Preservation Group, in which Tony and Gloria Blackman and their four sons are leading figures. Some fourteen AEC vehicles are owned by the Blackman family, including this one and ranging from a 1935 Bradford 8.8-litre Regent converted for snowplough duty to a Western Welsh Renown that had been an exhibit at the 1964 Commercial Motor Show. The Group as a whole owns about 100 vehicles, including other AECs such as ex-Liverpool vehicles, thus justifying the title though it is by no means exclusive to the areas of the two rivers. (Tony Blackman)

This mobile crane was bought new by a Scunthorpe heavy contractor and registered UFW 477, implying a 1959 date. It passed to Hewson Smith & Co (later Roland and John Smith), of Scamblesby, Lincs, in 1963, who used it until three or four years ago. Despite the rather sad appearance in Brian Goulding's photograph of last November, both the main AV470 engine and that in the NCK crane are said by Roland Smith to be still "on the button". The latter unit is noteworthy as being a four-cylinder unit with AEC-Maudslay badges, evidently one of the AV312 type built to similar design to the AV470 for industrial uses. The official photograph of a similar vehicle in chassis cab form Brian has also provided, shows that, in running gear and cab lower half, it is basically an AEC Mercury converted to 6 x 4, using two Mercury rear axles, even though carrying AWD badges. What Alan Townsin finds particularly interesting is that this is a Vickers-Armstrongs of Newcastle-upon-Tyne photograph and it seems logical to conclude that the very strong welded steel frame was produced at the

Elswick or Scotswood works well used to such work, where he had been apprenticed as part of his engineering training in 1944-47. Moreover, there is a much earlier and more important historic link, for AEC's original Walthamstow works began in its very early Vanguard days before AEC existed by assembling MOC (Motor Omnibus Construction) chassis which used Armstrong Whitworth parts supplied from the same Elswick works and reputedly largely of A. W. design – see page 26. Just to tie another strand of the personal connection, Alan's father was Commercial Manager of Armstrong Saurer, which built oil-engined vehicles to Saurer design at what was then still Armstrong Whitworth's Scotswood works in the early 'thirties, as part of a long career with the Armstrong Whitworth and, later, Vickers-Armstrongs organisations. An informative article by Nick Baldwin in Vintage Commercial Vehicle Magazine, July 1992, reveals that a financial link between Vickers-Armstrongs and AWD began in 1962. The more recent AWD which took over Bedford in 1987 is not related.(B. Goulding, Vickers-Armstrongs)

The Mark V goods range had its own distinctive style, set by the elimination of the 'bulge' cab front profile which, to some eyes at least, had made the Mercury range (and also the attempt to modernise the Mark III goods models with a similar front panel) seem a regression to something reminiscent of bus styles of the mid-'thirties that had been made obsolete by models such as the RT. The Mammoth Major eight-wheeled example seen below dated from 1962, and started life as a Guinness tanker before being converted to a recovery vehicle by Graham Lenox of Stanford-le-Hope, Essex. Sadly, he was one of those who lost their lives in the Spirit of Free Enterprise ferry disaster but the Mammoth Major was donated to Tony Blackman by Mrs Lenox in his memory. It is seen here towing JX 9106, a Regal I dating from 1946 originally operated by Hebble Motor Services Ltd and converted by that concern itself also as a towing vehicle, the Weymann body being shortened accordingly – it was in course of restoration at the time. The body design on this batch of vehicles, as with other Weymann Regals of the time, including the London Transport 14T12 class, had a profile with overhung destination box thought to have been originally devised for East Midland.   (Tony Blackman)

Most Mandator Mark V models were articulated tractive units and the vehicle shown above is a typical late example with AV690 engine, dating from 1965 and having the larger AEC letters applied to the radiator grille in the manner then standard, though usually at a lower level and with letters arranged horizontally. The repositioning of the nearside windscreen wiper was a logical change for an artic driver in particular needs good vision close to the nearside corner of his vehicle. Purchased by Daniel Stewart from the original owner, Munro Transport of Aberdeen, 10 years ago and restored by him, BRS 958C is seen at Wainfleet in June 1991, being now owned by Kevin Dennis.   (W. J. Taylor)

One of the surprises of the late 'eighties was the way in which ex-London Transport Routemaster buses were placed in service by a variety of operators who decided to revert to crew operation as a response to the onset of deregulation. The Scottish Bus Group subsidiary Clydeside Scottish played a leading part in this, for trials with a borrowed vehicle in 1985 led to orders from three of the SBG companies totalling 137 buses. Among Clydeside Scottish's allocation was RM37, one of the early production vehicles dating from 1959, seen in Glasgow in September 1988. Such vehicles have given good service, underlining the model's durability, but the type's future is bound to be limited even where conductor operation continues to be favoured unless the relatively modest need for replacement parts after so many years can be met. Even London Regional Transport's re-engining programme has yet to prove itself in terms of maintaining previous standards of long-term reliability. However the refurbishing of most of the RML-type buses, coupled with the fitting of Iveco or Cummins engines, makes it probable that the Routemaster will remain a familiar sight in London for some time to come. (W. S. N. Barlow)

One of the more remarkable survivors is the prototype right-hand drive Sabre coach, with rear-mounted V8 engine – AEC's swan-song in terms of a completely new engine design even though it was marketed as the British Leyland 800-series unit. It was the most powerful British coach of its time with 247 bhp when announced at the 1968 Show, where a left-hand chassis was shown, yet little was heard until the right-hand vehicle shown appeared complete with Eastern Coach Works body at the 1970 Show. The 800-series engine was under-developed, even though promising, and the project was not pursued, though two Cummins-engined chassis were also built, making a total of four – one going to Australia, receiving a Denning body, and one to South America. The ECW coach was sold to Best & Sons of Wembley, for some reason receiving an Oldham registration number CBU 636J, but in more recent times has passed to Kemp's Coaches of Chillenden near Canterbury, re-registered as SAB 784. It is seen at the 1990 AEC Society rally in Nottingham. (B. Goulding)

By March 1969, when the last two Regents of all to enter service took the road for Pontypridd Urban District Council (later Taff Ely Borough Council), AEC's long and distinguished run as a manufacturer of double-deckers had ended. As it turned out, these last vehicles were of the mediumweight 2MD3RA type, the last two of the more numerous heavy-duty type going to Douglas Corporation in December 1968, all four of these having Willowbrook forward-entrance bodywork. Taff Ely 7 (UTG 312G) now preserved, has travelled widely since withdrawal and is seen when visiting the Severn Valley Railway in Kidderminster in October 1989. (M. Fowler)

With its double-deck business gone, just as urban operators were turning back to such vehicles with renewed strength, AEC became, more than ever before in peacetime, primarily a goods vehicle manufacturer. The Ergomatic cab standardised by the Leyland group for almost all forward-control models from 1965 production offered improved comfort and internal quietness, as well as tilt-cab accessibility, though it proved rust-prone and quite often caused the premature scrapping of mechanically sound vehicles. The Mandator tractive

unit was particularly popular, initially with AV691 engine. This fine shot dating from 1969 shows XMP 857G, one of the fleet (another photo shows nine similar vehicles) operated by the Lye Trading Co Ltd, negotiating its way through an awkward turn near its depot in Lye among the rolling Black Country hills. At that date, the Construction and Use Regulations as revised in 1965 set minimum limits for the spread of axles bordering on the impractical and hence a 32-ton artic had to have the semi-trailer bogie set well back. (AEC)

The main emphasis on AEC bus business was placed on the rear-engined Swift model from its introduction in 1964, but as with several other first-generation passenger models of this layout, operator reaction was mixed. They often tended to be better liked in fleets serving smaller towns and Great Yarmouth Transport Ltd, as it is now known, is believed to be the last municipally-owned fleet in Britain still operating in everyday revenue-earning service AEC buses which it bought new. A fleet of twelve, all with AH505 engines and Eastern Coach Works bodywork (built 10 miles along the coast, at Lowestoft), was delivered in 1973, by which date the Swift was under threat of extinction by the all-pervading Leyland National. There is no plan to withdraw them in the foreseeable future. This one was photographed in April 1989. (W. S. N. Barlow)

AEC's most widely successful passenger model in its later years was the Reliance, especially the 11- and 12-metre versions. Quite a bit of this success was due to the adoption as a standard option of the ZF six-speed synchromesh gearbox with the AH590 and later large-capacity engines which permitted relaxed 70 mph cruising when most competitors' models were still tending to sound frantic at about 60 mph or so. This scene at the 1991 AEC Society's rally shows, on the right, HLP 10C, a 1965 example with Harrington Grenadier bodywork originally owned by Surrey Motors of Sutton (an always immaculately-kept AEC fleet) but sold to Premier Travel of Cambridge, which had standardised on the Reliance for its extensive express network, and ran until 1980. It was acquired by G. J. Cochrane of Ely for preservation in 1983 and in 1990 restored to Premier pre-1974 livery. Alongside is WEB 409T with Plaxton Supreme IV body, new to Premier in 1979 and based on one of the last Reliance chassis built. When Premier was taken over by Cambus in 1990 it was transferred to Cambridge Coach Services and retrimmed for continued use; HLP 10C is also operated under charter to this concern, successors to its former owner. (A. A. Townsin)

Unseen by many people because they tend to be confined to airfields, the RAF's fleet of Mammoth Major six-wheelers maintain a tradition extending back half a century to the old 854 days. Although quite a number have been sold off, including several that served in the Gulf, the fleet still in use includes not only refuellers but specialist vehicles such as this pair seen at Brize Norton in November 1991, equipped for de-icing aircraft wings and tailplanes and based on the same 2TG6RB chassis as the refuellers. At the rear are a Zwicky pump and an oil-fired boiler to heat the de-icing fluid, dispensed via 75ft. hydraulic platforms. The vehicle on the right has a Bison front panel, replacing the original because of the common corrosion problem.
(B. Goulding)

End of the line. What is believed to be the last Mammoth Major 8-wheeler has been located for preservation, marking an association of the make extending with this chassis configuration back to 1934 and nowadays followed by commercial vehicle makers all over the world. This is understood to have been the last AEC goods vehicle built, the chassis being delivered on 5th January 1978 to Lex Tillotson, the dealers — in itself appropriate as Tillotson had been AEC dealers since the early 'thirties. Its first operator was Sugruie Bros of Watford on heavy contract work, though latterly relegated to a site in Kent after the rear bogie gave trouble. It then ran for Bath Plant of Southampton with a container-type body for a year. It spent the latter part of its working life on timber haulage, fitted with an Atlas crane, firstly with Postle Haulage and then with Moodie's Transport, Chazey Heath, near Reading. It was found in a yard near Oxford last year by Kevin Dennis, who has added it to his collection of preserved lorries.
(W. J. Taylor)

Companhia Carris di Ferro de Lisboa, better known as CCFL or simply 'Carris', was established as Lisbon Electric Tramways Ltd, originally registered in London, though in more recent years Portuguese-owned. Its initial fleet of six buses, six single-deckers on AEC Regent chassis, doubtless chosen allowing for the anticipated heavy loading of standing passengers, dated from 1940 and a similar pattern, though using the left-hand-drive preselective Mark III chassis, continued as the fleet expanded in 1948-50, after which a switch was made to double-deckers. Number 255, dating from 1954, was typical of 80 such buses with Weymann bodywork supplied up to 1956. It is seen in its last months of service heeling over at an alarming angle when negotiating Place Comercio, Lisbon, in October 1982, producing an effect like a live-load tilt test.   (Brian King)

AEC world-wide 1 – Portugal

Happily, when an example of the Lisbon Regent III was secured for preservation by John Shearman, it was the same number 255, seen at Coimbra, Portugal, en route for Britain in April 1983. Alongside is one of the municipality of Coimbra's two Regent V buses, almost identical to the Lisbon examples and having UTIC bodywork, a mere 20 years old compared to 255's age of 29 years. Even after 'retirement' as a preserved bus, 255 can still give an exhilarating ride.
(John Shearman)

One of CCFL's Regent V models dating from 1961, seen when almost new outside the Monastery of Jeronimus. Number 382 was one of thirteen with forward-entrance body built by the operator but to Weymann design. Subsequently some almost identical-looking vehicles were built as integral vehicles by UTIC using Regent V chassis parts. A few are still retained for staff transport and other special duties.   (AEC)

It is reckoned that well over 2,500 AEC vehicles are still in service in Portugal, making it nowadays the most concentrated habitat for the make in the world and perhaps now the main user country. Much of this is due to the continued devotion of the UTIC concern, enthusiastic agents since the 'fifties, taking up the concept of the integral coach based on the Monocoach underframe almost as soon as the model went into production in 1954 and producing 'new'-looking examples by rebodying as recently as 1990, as well as Reliance and Swift versions. Three generations of UTIC-AEC are seen in this view in Villa Real, taken by Paul Richman in June 1991, as were all on the following three pages. The vehicle on the right is a 1990 rebodied example.

Rodoviaria Nacional, a Portuguese equivalent of the National Bus Company, using the initials RN as its fleetname, quoted its AEC fleet at 1,915 out of a total of 3,017 full-sized buses and coaches in the summary in the 1991-92 issue of The Little Red Book. Seen here at Tomor is an example of the final original types of UTIC-AEC, called the Europa.

The RN fleet also includes various AEC goods vehicles, including this Marshal breakdown truck with local design of cab, apparently not of the tilting type, seen at the RN depot for the Setubal area.

Alcantara Transport Co-operative runs a fleet of varied AEC goods models. Three generations are visible in this scene in the Lisbon dock area – a pre-tilt cab Mercury/Monarch (export Mercury-type models were generally called Monarch) with Portuguese cab, a tilt-cab Monarch, and a Marathon, the latter a Leyland but counting as a member of the AEC family by virtue of the AEC-derived TL12 engine as well as assembly of many at Southall works until it closed.

Another Alcantara AEC – a Mandator with container semi-trailer – at work in the Lisbon docks.

A little battered but still active, this locally-cabbed Monarch of an anonymous operator was also seen in the Lisbon dock area. Export versions of the model known in Britain as the Mercury were given the Monarch name, evidently because Ford was using Mercury as a car name at the time. Presumably AEC was able to show it had established rights to the name in Britain going back to 1930. The cab is by UTIC

This example of a UTIC-AEC of the mid-to-late 'fifties with original bodywork was still in service with a local operator in June 1991 in the Viseu area.

Seen in Oporto, this UTIC-AEC of Gondomarense has bodywork of circa 1980 though the chassis or underframe is believed to be earlier.

This smart and up-to-date-looking bus owned by the municipal transport undertaking of Nazaré, a town north-west of Lisbon, has one of the earliest left-hand Monocoach underframes – number 23 – dating from 1956, with a new UTIC body dating from 1989. It is seen at the depot in June 1991.

2 – Malta

The island of Malta is always a likely bet for interesting old vehicles and AECs are no exception. These photographs were taken during a July 1985 visit by Brian Goulding but it is likely that most, or others like them, are still in use. This Mammoth Major V tipper driven by John Cadwarner, its owner, was at work near St. Pauls Bay. Many tilt-cab AEC models are also still in use, all bought second-hand from the UK. The odd 0853 Matador is also still to be seen.

(Centre) When London Transport's Merlin and Swift single-deckers were withdrawn after relatively short lives many of them re-entered service in locations spread far across the world. Malta was to be the new home for a number of Swifts from 1981 and one is seen here at Mellieha, with original outline unchanged but with a characteristically Maltese combination of traditional-style lining-out with a 'modern' grille applied to the front panels. This one was SMS 810, with MCW body, dating from January 1972.

(Below) The ingenuity of Maltese operators in marrying up combinations of engines and other units means that vehicles may not always be what they seem, but the emphasis on display of the AEC initials as well as the winged version of the badge on these two vehicles seems to convey a sense of pride. Both are evidently based on Mercury-range chassis, possibly second-hand from the UK. Duple influence is evident in the frontal styling of the 1971 vehicle shown below at Ramla Bay, with windscreen of post-1968 design though the grille is more akin to a slightly earlier pattern as used in Britain. The vehicle on the service linking Valetta with Gozo Ferry (below right) has bodywork of a typically Maltese style with strong American car influence from the 'fifties era of wide 'dollar grin' grilles and tail fins. It entered service in Malta in 1965. Both these widely different vehicles have bodywork by Aquilina.

3 – Greece

The first ten examples of the 670-type Ranger, designed as a left-hand drive model, were supplied to Athens in 1931, having 110-bore petrol engines, centre-line transmission layout and 19ft. wheelbase. What is almost certainly one is seen (top), posed near the Acropolis.   (AEC)

The Athens Electric Transport Co became a regular AEC customer and in 1938 some 60 Regals with Metro-Cammell 32ft. x 8ft. full-fronted metal-framed bodywork were supplied. They had an unusual version of what was basically the 8.8-litre engine, but linered down to 103mm bore while retaining the 142mm stroke, giving a capacity of just over 7 litres, apparently to suit local taxation rules. Power output would have been less than a 7.7 but it should have proved a very robust unit. Fluid transmission and 19ft. wheelbase were other features.   (N. G. Tuckwell collection)

Though Greece was not so prominent as a market for AEC vehicles in later years, this Regal VI was posed in 1966 near the same spot as the picture at the top of the page. It was one of 45 for A. L. Brissis Konst, operating in Athens, assembled and bodied locally.   (AEC)

4 – Cyprus

The British influence is still clearly evident in the use of the left-hand rule of the road and such details as the style of registration plates, but the Greek history remains dominant in much of the island. Even so, this tilt-cab Mammoth Major, rather battered but still in service, could well be a home-market example but for the Greek lettering in the background of this view in Limassol old docks in 1983 taken during a visit by Brian Goulding, when he took all the photographs on this page and overleaf. It was probably imported second-hand from Britain, as are most AECs in Cyprus.

Lefkaritis Bros have operated a large fleet of British vehicles and especially AECs for many years – Kallis Lefkaritis has been an AEC Society member since its founding days. This coach, seen at St. George's Monastery, is based on one of the last Ranger chassis, one of 30 stored at the Nottingham ex-AEC depot until the early 'eighties, ten of which were converted from left-hand to right-hand, and the front axle set back as shown, it is believed in Cyprus.

An early Mercury with local derivative of the standard cab well laden with sacks near the port of Limassol.

This Mandator Mark V artic tanker looked quite well cared-for, apart from some minor dents – it was seen at the Lefkaritis depot in Larnaca.

Cyprus's climate appears to help to preserve discarded vehicles. These three 854-type aircraft refuellers with 'condemned' markings at one of Lefkaritis's 'camps' looked as if they hadn't moved for some time, seeming basically complete, and reasonably rust-free though the disintegration of the nearest vehicle's cab door suggests that wood rot had set in. Beyond them are a Bedford QL and a Mammoth Major III refueller.

Another early Monarch of the Mercury-based export type, a long-wheelbase version, with cab as often fitted to contemporary examples in Britain. This is another member of the Lefkaritis fleet, also at the Larnaca depot.

5 – Iraq

6 – Iran

The Middle east grew immensely in importance as a market for AEC buses in the 'fifties. Baghdad Passenger Transport Service based its policy on London Transport advice, beginning with 100 Regal III models with Park Royal bodywork in 1951, though the chassis differed from LT standards, and also all previous left-hand drive examples of this model, in having crash gearboxes and thus being of type 9631A. Seen above is one of a second 100 supplied in 1953; a third followed in 1956-57.   (Park Royal)

In 1958 Teheran took delivery of a remarkably large first order for 250 Regent V buses, of type D2LA with 11.3-litre engines, Monocontrol transmission and Park Royal bodywork. Two well-laden examples are seen here in service in 1962, in company with some Mercedes-Benz cars. Baghdad had also switched to double-deckers, following with 100 rather similar buses a few months later and further orders from both undertakings, generally of 100 or 200 at a time, followed up to 1967. It would be interesting to know if any survive from either fleet.   (AEC)

7 – Malaya

This photograph conveys the atmosphere of the heydays of the British colonial regime, with architecture which married oriental ideas with Victorian British neo-Gothic, an AEC double-deck bus and even a bus stop sign of pattern very like that then common in 'the home country'. It was taken early in 1950 – towards the end of that era so far as Malaya was concerned – and shows one of three Regent III 9612E models with Park Royal bodywork, all basically of home-market pattern, though this particular five-bay body style was more often associated with other chassis makes. The location is the railway station, Kuala Lumpar. The operator, General Transport Company, had adopted an appropriately London-style bulls-eye motif.   (PRV)

8 – Hong Kong

A much larger market for Regent chassis in the Far East emerged in 1963, when the Kowloon Motor Bus Co (1933) Ltd began taking delivery of a special 21ft. 6in.-wheelbase version of the Regent V. This concern, operating the New Territories' area forming part of the colony of Hong Kong, but on the Chinese mainland, required a fleet of high-capacity double-deckers and although previously a Daimler user, turned to AEC, which could offer a chassis derived from the Regal III of similar wheelbase. Although this was intended as a single-decker, it had been built to withstand gross overloading as well as use on poor roads, notably in Africa. The initial order was for 110, but a further 100 followed, delivery of all 210 being spread over the period up to 1966. The engine was the AV690 11.3-litre and Monocontrol transmission was fitted, while the bodywork was built in Hong Kong from parts supplied from Britain, mostly by Metal Sections – seating was provided for about 80 people, varying from batch to batch, with total capacity a nominal 120 or so, frequently exceeded. John Shearman resolved to bring one back to Britain for preservation to join his ex-Lisbon Regent III and A165 of the Kowloon fleet is seen in the photograph he took at the main entrance gate of the former AEC works in July 1987, 21 years after its chassis had been built there, on its way to the Oxford Bus Museum. Another is preserved in Newcastle, NSW.

9 – Uganda

This photograph graphically illustrates the uncertainties faced by the designer of a bus for service where theoretical load limitations are unlikely to be observed. The idea of carrying luggage on the roof is very old established but the provision of a reinforced area with a sturdy frame round it was an invitation accepted to good effect by the users of this Regal III 9621E 21ft. 6in.-wheelbase model with Park Royal bodywork, one of twelve dating from 1955 for Uganda Transport Co Ltd. With something like 100 passengers aboard, it is not difficult to visualise how the enquiry from Kowloon Motor Bus for a 21ft. 6in. version of the Regent to carry 120 passengers for service in Hong Kong could be based on a similar chassis frame, suitably adapted.   (AEC)

10 – Zimbabwe

Much the same principle, applied to shorter vehicles, can be seen on these two Ranger models of Tamburayi Bus Service in what was then Rhodesia, of which the photograph was received by AEC in 1960. This generation of Ranger, in effect a Mercury adapted for passenger applications, proved popular in such conditions, the goods-type frame allowing more ground clearance. It is thought that some may survive in rural areas.   (AEC)

AEC was well established in South Africa by the 'thirties. Among the most interesting individual vehicles of that period was this Renown of Johannesburg Municipal Tramways. Fitted with an 8.8-litre oil engine and Metro-Cammell 64-seat body, it dated from 1935. Records show that a chassis with the same number, 664253, had been built as a show exhibit but was dismantled, though O664253 (the 'O' prefix signifying oil engine in the manner by then usual) was built for Johannesburg soon after and it seems quite possible that some parts at least were re-used. It appears from this photograph, evidently taken some years later, that the body, to the Jo'burg derivative of Metro-Cammell's standard style of the period, was 8ft. wide though the chassis was evidently 7ft. 6in. Semi-floating rear axles were still standard for the Renown at that date, though a fully-floating rear bogie was introduced that year for the 664T trolleybus and was adopted for Renown chassis a year or two later.   (Photo supplied by Paul Fox)

11 – South Africa

In later years, South African requirements led to the development of an AEC bus model specific to that part of the world. This was the Kudu, which was in effect a Regal Mk VI chassis with an AV690 vertical engine mounted on the front overhang, the objective being to move the engine into a position in which it could operate in relatively clean air when running on dirt roads. Underfloor-engined models had been found to be unsatisfactory because of the dust thrown up by the front wheels. On the other hand the long wheelbase and set-back front axle allowed high-capacity bodywork – a seating capacity of 60 was usual – and driver-supervised loading. Seen here is a very early example, possibly the prototype, operated by the municipality of Benoni and with body by Africa Body & Coach, a subsidiary of PUTCO, South Africa's largest company undertaking. The black exhaust smoke is a rather surprising feature of a picture used by AEC for publicity purposes, suggesting that the engine might have been incorrectly set – engines on AEC buses for Johannesburg were derated to suit the 5,000ft. altitude and this would also have been necessary for other places similarly located, to give a clear exhaust.   (AEC)

(Above) Over the years, AEC's interests in South Africa were handled by various concerns but from 1959 the construction of an assembly plant at Durban by AEC Vehicles (SA) Ltd was linked to body and finishing shops of J. H. Plane & Co Ltd of Johannesburg. Two Marshal models with concrete mixer equipment illustrate the South African variant of the standard cab of that period when lined up for photography outside the Plane plant. (AEC)

A Super Mammoth tractor, using the huge AV1100 engine of some 18-litre capacity, seen outside the J. H. Plane works – at least one example of this model was supplied to South African Railways. The photograph dates from about 1964 and an intriguing vehicle in the background is an ERF which would appear to be a pre-1948 model, still in smart condition. (AEC)

Among the oldest AEC vehicles believed to be still in normal service in South Africa is this vehicle, evidently a Mammoth Major Mark III though it has a Mandator grille badge, which was found derelict on a farm at Bredasdorp early in 1990 but purchased by a local operator and put back into use – the photograph, taken near Piketberg by Wally Greig, dates from August 1990. The cab design has some slight resemblances to the 'new look' version of the Mark III goods range as built in Britain from about 1955, but adopted to give a wrap-round windscreen effect in a style not seen in Britain and suggesting an early 'sixties date.

The PUTCO fleet of Kudu buses was once reckoned to approach 2,000 but was greatly reduced in later years, partly by competition from smaller vehicles and reduction in subsidies, though still amounting to several hundred. Some have recently received major rebuilds, making their future seem quite bright. A typical vehicle, with the square-cut type of body by BUSAF, the South African associate of MCW, is seen in this photograph taken by Brian Goulding in March 1991 at PUTCO's Johannesburg depot. Chassis frame breakage over the front axle tended to be a problem when they were operated on rough roads; the weight of the engine mounted well ahead of the axle would not help. Nowadays they are kept off such duty.

In for refurbishing at the former J. H. Plane depot now owned by AAD, successors to Leyland South Africa, at the time of Brian Goulding's visit in 1991 were ten Kudu buses of the South African Army dating from 1963-64. The bodywork, by Brockhouse (SA), has distinct echoes of the BET standard designs of that period, probably using imported parts – the chassis, of type 2S2RA, has AV690 engine and Monocontrol epicyclic gearbox. Note the Leyland lettering applied diagonally on the grille. (B. Goulding)

This 1960 Regent V is one of two retained in the Johannesburg fleet, converted to open top. The BUSAF body is very similar to those on Guy Victory J chassis in the Cape Town fleet and is seen on 3rd January 1992 as painted for the Christmas season the previous month. It nowadays has a Gardner 6LXB engine in place of the original AV690. The James Hall Museum in Johannesburg includes another Regent V of 1956/7, an RT and two BUT six-wheel double-deck trolleybuses. (K. Froud)

This view of the AEC Road Train sent to Australia in 1934 when new shows the aptness of the name, with some 24 wheels divided between the tractor and the two Dyson trailers. The utilitarian appearance was emphasised by the front mounting of the two spare wheels, with the vehicle's identity conveyed only by the AEC triangle. It was a product of the work on cross-country vehicles carried out by Hardy as described on page 33, the model number being thought to be 851. (AEC)

12 – Australia

The complexity of the Road Train tractor as built for Australia is conveyed by this drawing. The original engine was an 8.8-litre Ricardo-head unit of basically the then standard specification, with the usual output of 130bhp at 2,000 rpm. The drive was taken via a four-speed and reverse main gearbox (probably the standard 'crash' unit of the time), through a three-speed auxiliary box mounted amidships to the rearmost axle and then via short intermediate propeller shafts to the other three, the vehicle thus being an 8 x 8. The foremost and rearmost axles steered and each pair of axles were sprung, bogie fashion, to allow the contours of very rough ground to be accommodated. The two trailers were similarly sprung and the geometry of the whole outfit was so arranged that each would follow quite precisely in the tracks of the tractor, thus justifying the description 'road train' and giving the trailers the benefit of the smoothing-out effect of the tractor's wheels.

The combination's rated payload was quite conservative, at 15 tons, though clearly intended to allow for the problems of rough terrain, and was exceeded considerably at times. The tractor itself weighed 7 tons 19cwt in chassis form and the load capacity (payload plus body) was only 3 tons 16cwt, but a clue to its capabilities is given by the tractive effort figure, expressed locomotive-style, of 15,000lb. The trailers were each rated at 6 tons payload.

A Westinghouse compressed air brake system, rare on a British goods vehicle in those days, was provided, though only the two centre axles of the tractor were braked. The control system allowed for the brakes on the rearmost trailer to be applied first, then the first trailer and finally those on the tractor, preventing trailer over-run. The radiator was located high up behind the engine, with a huge slow-speed fan driven by belt from an auxiliary shaft on the engine which also drove the compressor for the brakes. The normal engine fan was retained to circulate air round the engine and the occupants of the cab.

A prototype road train, but with petrol engine, had been built by AEC in 1929 under the auspices of the British Overseas Mechanical Transport Committee and tested in the Gold Coast (now Ghana) in Africa. In the late 1930s similar vehicles are understood to have been sent to the Soviet Union, and it would be interesting to discover if anything is known of their fate. Fortunately the Australian vehicle survived and has been preserved, as shown overleaf.

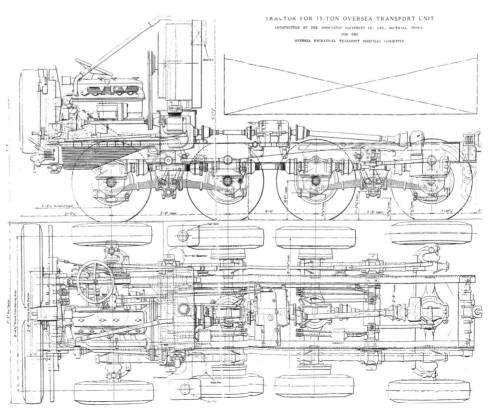

The Road Train entered service on arrival in Australia at the end of April 1934, starting with a run from Adelaide to Alice Springs, over part of which there was no road. By December it had covered 10,000 miles with no mechanical defects and in the next ten years, operating out of Alice Springs it is estimated it covered 770,000 miles. Starting proved difficult in winter as seems to have been common with AEC-Ricardo engines, but it became standard practice to shovel the embers of camp fires under the engine or if possible to park on a downward slope. It was reckoned the tractor, with an overall bottom gear ratio of 94.5 to 1, could 'haul anything' and if terrain was difficult, it could get through itself and then haul the trailers using the winch and cable also provided. When normal roads in the Northern Territory were closed during the War with the threat of invasion by the Japanese, it supplied food and necessities to small settlements throughout the region. The biggest load was two railway carriages weighing 45 tons, taken from Alice Springs to Larrimah for use by the Red Cross after the Japanese had bombed Darwin. Plans to restore it began when it was found in Darwin in 1964, and after passing through the hands of enthusiast individuals it was acquired by the Museums and Art Galleries Board of the Northern Territories, who supplied these photographs of the restored vehicle when nearing completion. The original engine was found to be irrepairable, with broken con-rods and a hole in the crankcase, so a 1948 7.7-litre unit from a bus was fitted and the Museum's workshops handed the tractor over in October 1990 and it is now on display in Alice Springs. One of the trailers has been found and it is hoped to restore this too, if the funds to be raised by an appeal allow. We are indebted to Graham Edge and Jared Archibald of the Museum & Art Galleries of the Northern Territories, Darwin, for information and illustrations.

This Regent chassis, number O6614438, dating from March 1937, remained in continuous public service for 41½ years, claimed as a record for an Australian double-decker and pretty hard to beat anywhere. It was placed in service by the Department of Road Transport and Tramways (DRTT) of the Government of New South Wales, responsible for public transport in Sydney and also the smaller city of Newcastle, NSW. It has a body by Waddington, one of the first batch of steel-framed bodies in the fleet and having the characteristic outline with steeply-sloping profile which was to remain typical of Australian double-deckers. The chassis was of basically standard Regent specification of the time, with 7.7-litre engine and crash gearbox.

It ran 579,163 miles with DRTT in Sydney before sale in August 1953 to an independent operator, Linsley Bros of Wallsend, which appropriately, as judged by a native of Newcastle-upon-Tyne, is a suburb of Newcastle, NSW, and then on to Allome's Bus Service of Garden Suburb in the same city, not being retired until that concern ceased trading in September 1978. It was under restoration (since completed) to original condition by David Wilson when seen in this photo at the bus and truck museum at Tempe, NSW in July 1987. Oddly enough, another well-known Regent with an exceptionally long service life by British standards, the former Gosport & Fareham No. 35 (BOR 767), which remained in service for 30 years beginning in 1936 and also, happily, preserved has chassis number O6614417, just 21 numbers earlier and probably contemporary in time – see page 32. (C. Goodsell)

Another remarkable DRTT vehicle operating in Sydney from the same period is trolleybus 19, dating from 1937, one of a batch of ten AEC 664T chassis with bodywork by Ritchie Bros, seating 60 with rear entrance and front exit in the same manner as used in Newcastle in Britain. Indeed the body styling was closer to British practice – quite similar to Newcastle on Tyne vehicles of 1935 - than applied with the motor bus standard, apart from the 8ft. body width and angled end windows in the lower deck. The vehicles, together with eleven similar Leylands, remained in service until 1959 when trolleybus operation ceased. Number 19 was found in derelict condition in 1979 and obtained by the Sydney Tramway Museum, being restored by the apprentice training college of the State Railway Authority. It is seen at Tempe in December 1988 – it is hoped to erect overhead for it at the Tramway Museum at Loftus, Sydney. (C. Goodsell)

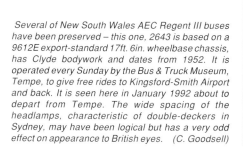

Several of New South Wales AEC Regent III buses have been preserved – this one, 2643 is based on a 9612E export-standard 17ft. 6in. wheelbase chassis, has Clyde bodywork and dates from 1952. It is operated every Sunday by the Bus & Truck Museum, Tempe, to give free rides to Kingsford-Smith Airport and back. It is seen here in January 1992 about to depart from Tempe. The wide spacing of the headlamps, characteristic of double-deckers in Sydney, may have been logical but has a very odd effect on appearance to British eyes. (C. Goodsell)

Canberra favoured the variant of the Regal III with 7.7-litre engine and crash gearbox and this example, chassis number O682213, placed in service in 1949, is seen in Canberra after restoration in September 1989. Bodywork is by Commonwealth Engineering and the vehicle is preserved by Canberra Transport Department, together with a Reliance. (C. Goodsell)

The underfloor-engined single-decker generally displaced the double decker for new deliveries to city fleets in Australia after the early 1950s, to permit driver-only operation, passenger capacity being maintained by increasing the number standing. American influence on public transport policy in Australia was becoming more evident and the styling of the Clyde body on this Regal IV 9823E placed in service in the NSW Government fleet in 1959 has similarities to the American-designed PCC tramcar – it remained in service until 1978 and is seen in January 1989 on a special service for Motorfest 89 – it had been restored a year earlier, running on 'vintage registration'. The Sydney Harbour Bridge is just visible – as is a Regal III – in the background. (C. Goodsell)

Lindsay's of Coffs Harbour, NSW, operates these Regal VI models dating from 1963 and originally owned by the government transport service in Perth, Western Australia. They were transported by rail across country and are in daily use as school buses but the New South Wales Government has introduced a new regulation requiring a maximum age limit of 15 years and this will enforce the withdrawal of all AECs. (C. Goodsell)

Though considerably disguised by body modifications, this is a former London Transport Merlin, MBA174, with MCW body of 1968 – originally a Red Arrow bus, though early in its life transferred to other duties. It was sold to Rowe's Coach Tours Ltd, of Plumpton, near Sydney, in 1976, later to Kirklands of Lismore, about 500 miles north and then Winchesters of Eureka nearby, with whom it is seen in this June 1991 photograph.
(C. Goodsell)

Melbourne operated large fleets of Regal buses of Marks III, IV and VI, examples of all of which have been preserved. The last AEC in service for that city's fleet is seen shortly before withdrawal in October 1989 at Sandringham depot, regular driver Alex Johnston doing a battery check. The bodywork, built to Melbourne's strange-looking requirements, is by Freighter, and the Regal VI chassis has 11.3-litre engine and automatic transmission.
(B. Goulding)

Adelaide is another Australian city which took AEC buses in quite large numbers from the 'thirties onwards. Here again, the emphasis was on single-deckers from the 'fifties and this Swift, one of three now operated by Sawtell Coaches and seen in June 1991 is representative of the final type with vertical exhaust at the rear. Remarkably, they were rebuilt to narrow the width by $2\frac{1}{2}$ in, to meet NSW regulations. (C. Goodsell)

Many old AEC goods models are held in store by Roy Brown, founder of R. W. Brown & Son of Newcastle, NSW, which held an AEC franchise until Leyland closed down in Australia. Here a bonneted Mandator Mark III is seen in a recent photograph alongside a Monarch, the latter having been in the fleet of Newcastle Haulage & Transport, the haulage division of the same concern. (Tony Petch)

This Merryweather fire engine with 100ft. turntable ladder on what was basically a Regent III chassis is similar to those built for various British users. It is seen on an uncharacteristically wet 1st January 1989 at the NSW Fire Department Museum at Penrith, NSW. (C. Goodsell)

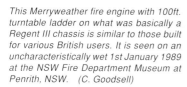

This Mandator III has an A221, six-speed overdrive main gearbox and two-speed auxiliary box – it is now privately owned. (Tony Petch)

Moving house in May 1990, Australian style, courtesy of a Mandator V, at Coffs Harbour, NSW. (C. Goodsell)

The Australian branches of several British automobile concerns, both car and commercial, always tended to be a law unto themselves. In 1964, a couple of years after the merger of AEC into the Leyland group, and before any significant sign of rationalisation of the truck range of the combined group became evident in Britain, AEC Australia introduced what was called the Mustang, model LGM4RA, marrying what amounted to a Mercury range chassis with AV470 engine and the LAD cab familiar on the Leyland Comet and heavy-duty goods ranges, many Albion and Dodge models but not elsewhere on an AEC. A six-speed gearbox and two-speed differential gave the speed range needed for Australian conditions. In Britain, the Mustang name had been applied to a twin-steer derivative of the Mercury range. Few are left, but Tony Petch photographed the out-of-use example seen below in August 1991.

Still in daily use is this Mammoth Major Mark V of Newcastle Haulage & Transport, NSW. It has a cab made by Hastings Deering of Sydney and has been repowered with an AEC AV760 engine and Fuller twin-stick 15-speed compound gearbox. (T. Petch)

Christchurch Transport Board's use of AEC buses began in quite dramatic fashion in 1936 with a delivery of four of the side-engined Q type, including number 225 as shown here, accompanied by six Regals. The Q must have been well regarded, as two more were ordered and entered service in 1938, evidently the last examples of the model to do so, though this may have been due to a time lapse between the delivery of the chassis and completion of the bodywork in the Board's own workshops, also responsible for the initial four and indeed all of the Christchurch AEC buses up to 1940, when six more Regals entered service. The Christchurch Q types were noteworthy in having the entrance in the front overhang (found only on London Transport's 5Q5 buses of 1936 among British-operated examples of the model) and an exit behind the rear axle. Examination of photographs, plus the combination of two doorways and a 39-seat capacity, strongly suggests that the Christchurch Q had a longer overhang at both front and rear than the standard British Q single-deckers of type O762, the overall length probably being nearer 30ft. than the 27ft. 6in. then in force as the maximum for a two-axle single-deck bus in Britain. Parts of three of the original 1936 batch passed to the Tramway Historical Society in Christchurch, and it is planned to rebuild one as a complete vehicle. A rather mysterious third late Q chassis, O762267 (the two placed in service being O762268 and 269)also went to New Zealand, possibly also intended for Christchurch, but is recorded as becoming a mobile crane with Wellington City Transport Engineers Department. We are indebted to the O. B. Monograph on New Zealand's AEC Buses for details of the above and other vehicles.   (Christchurch Transport Board)

13 – New Zealand

Christchurch Transport Board moved into a much bigger league as an AEC operator in 1952-54 when 95 Regal Mark IV of the 9821E type were delivered. The first 39 numerically had bodywork by Crossley and the rest Park Royal but all were to the same 42-seat front-entrance centre-exit style, based on an Park Royal export standard of the period. The photograph of the first vehicle (left) was taken by the late E. J. Smith, in those days employed in AEC's publicity department, just outside the AEC works entrance on 26th March 1952. Note the Crossley Coachwork transfer alongside the entrance step. A number of the Christchurch buses came back to Southall after bodying and before shipping and Alan Townsin, also at Southall at the time, well recalls the striking red and cream livery. This picture was taken to show the pram hooks on the front, a New Zealand characteristic which fascinated British transport journalists at the time. It is a happy coincidence that this bus is now restored (below) and in the Tramway Historical Society preserved fleet, being seen outside Moorhouse Avenue workshops in October 1988.   (David Jones)

From 1956, Christchurch switched to the Reliance, using a general chassis design very similar to the standard home market model in size and with the AH470 engine, but to an export specification with heavy-duty axles. Christchurch continued to favour the epicyclic gearbox, by this date in Monocontrol form and the chassis type was thus HMU2RA. There had been an initial batch of eighteen Reliance MU2RAE (an earlier export variant with heavy-duty front axle) in 1956-57, but 410, also now restored to a high standard, belonged to one of 20 vehicles, all of these having Park Royal bodywork seating 37 – a final ten of the HMU2RA also dating from 1958 were 42-seaters. It is preserved by the Tramway Historical Society, as is 452, which represents the final Reliance batch of 24 buses for this fleet, with New Zealand Motor Bodies coachwork, dating from 1963-64, seen on the right of the line-up of the three preserved Christchurch AEC buses below. (David Jones, Trevor Jones)

The final two AEC buses in the Christchurch fleet, 457 and 458, dating from 1977, were Swift 505 models of type 3MP2R, with bodywork by Hawke which is almost identical with the Eastern Coach Works bodywork on Great Yarmouth Corporation's Swifts in England, being built from ECW parts (see page 46). This is basically as more familiar on the Bristol RE chassis, of which Christchurch had 54, and this relationship is underlined on the Christchurch version as the vehicles have front-mounted radiators and hence are provided with grilles not unlike the style used on RE buses, though bearing the AEC winged badge. Note the ex-London RT just visible to the left of 457, in this view. There had been one previous Swift of the larger-engined 691 type with automatic transmission and an NZMB body in 1973, number 456, seen in the lower picture. This unique vehicle, originally badged as a Leyland, had the only example of this body design, called Commonwealth. (David Jones)

Auckland Transport Board operated a fleet of BUT trolleybuses which were of a unique type. When British United Traction was formed as a merger of AEC and Leyland interests in trolleybus and railcar manufacture, it was agreed that what were basically home-market models would be based on AEC designs and those specifically intended as export models would be of Leyland origin. A Leyland-designed single-deck model with entrance ahead of the front axle was produced, designated ETB1 but, in the event, an AEC-based model of similar layout was also built, this being the 9711T. The entire output of the type, 55 vehicles, was fitted with Metro-Cammell bodywork and entered service between 1949 and 1954, number 24 being seen at Lynfield terminus in January 1975. A similar vehicle, number 50, has been preserved by the Museum of Transport and Technology, Auckland.
(David Jones)

(Above) American influence was at one time quite strong in some New Zealand coach designs, particularly in the use of high-set shallow windows. This Reliance 470 with Nuttall body, was one of two dating from 1959 placed in service by Hawkes Bay Motor Co, of Napier, an operator which took delivery of 19 Reliance models of various types between 1955 and 1974. It is seen as running in the recent years for Mount Cook Line. (David Jones)

Another city fleet of AECs, snow represented by a smartly-restored example is Wellington City Transport, where number 322 represents a batch of 55 Reliance MU3RAE models with MCW bodywork dating from 1957, this photograph (left) being taken in December 1991. Three later vehicles are still in service up to May 1992 – number 371, a 1963 example with NZMB body seen (above left) being among them. (David Jones, Peter Rendall)

Not very many AEC passenger vehicles are still in service in New Zealand and some of them have been fitted with other makes of engine. One of the exceptions is Brian Bickmore's Reliance 691, type 6U3ZRE, new to Newmans Coachlines in 1973 and having 41-seat body by NZMB, purchased by Brian in July 1991. It is still completely standard and he intends to keep it that way. Newmans had fifteen Reliances new in the 1972-74 period, the fleet being divided between 691 models, allocated to the hillier North Island, and 505 models for the South Island fleet. (B. Bickmore)

Sales of AEC, or more correctly ACLO, buses to South America began in the 'twenties, but a specific landmark was the establishment of a regular flow of orders for the Co-operativa Bus Services based in Montevideo, Uruguay. The model chosen was the Regal, with 7.7-litre oil engine, right-hand steering being accepted despite the rule of the road. The first entered service in 1937 and by October of that year the AEC Gazette was able to announce that a total of 91 had been ordered, rising to 198 a year later, at the time the largest overseas AEC fleet. The exact date of this photograph from AEC archives is not known but it shows a Regal of pre-war specification and very probably dating from 1937 or soon after, when almost new.

When Mike Fenton visited Uruguay in September 1991, among several long-service ACLO Regal buses he photographed, this one, seen in Pando, about 25 miles north-east of Montevideo, was the most venerable. The body design, save for the addition of a front door and American style 'standee' windows above the main side windows, possibly later modifications, appears to be virtually the same as the vehicle shown above, and the chassis number, 06623056, confirms that the chassis dates from 1938. The owner, Carlos Marin Morales, had operated it for many years – his offer to sell it for $20,000 (US), was declined! (M. Fenton)

14 – Uruguay

In remarkably good order, even if lacking the radiator grille and bonnet side, was this Regal, 06624050, originally sold to C.I.T.A. of Montevideo in June 1946. Export orders for the Regal preceded those for home-market customers in the allocation of chassis numbers, when production was resumed after the war, and this was one of a run of 66 chassis exported via H. Torrendell, AEC's representation in Uruguay, who also had other batches of very early post-war Regals. The owner when seen in October 1991 was Oscar Castro, of San José de Mayo, about 55 miles west of Montevideo. The 33-seat body was described as Carrocerias Nacional by Senor Castro, but Mike does not have this firm listed among known Uruguayan builders and wonders if it might be another name for Carrocerias Independencia or even C.U.T.C.S.A. It was working a regular 25-mile run to Boca del Cufre.

South America was particularly in mind when the left-hand version of the Regal III, model O963, later 9631E, was introduced, for it was far more than a version of the home-market model with the driver's controls on the left. By making almost the entire chassis the opposite hand operators got the same benefits of accessibility – always a strong AEC feature – as with the right-hand model, not so on the competitive Leyland Tiger LOPS models, for example. The survival of many examples in Uruguay in particular 40 years or more later confirms the merit and durability of the design. The photographs on these two pages are selected from some taken by Mike Fenton during his visit to that country last September/October. This example, 0631E231 of 1949, also owned by Oscar Castro of San José, has bodywork of the same make as the Regal I on the previous page, but seating 37. Here again, the condition is described by Mike as superb, and the degree of originality in a 42-year-old vehicle working so far from its country of origin remarkable. The livery is orange, blue and white.

Sanchez No. 3 based on another 1949 chassis, 9631E236 appears to have received a locally-made radiator shell (the original pressings were vulnerable to minor damage, hence the aluminium version used later) with some distortion of the classic outline, with a more battered bonnet, but was clearly still going strong. The body design of this, builder unknown, vehicle has a more modern look, with fewer window pillars. The owner is José Alonso Sanchez of Tala, about 50 miles north of Montevideo.

Sanchez No. 4, based on what was originally a 7.7-litre engined right-hand chassis, 6821A634, of 1954, has a full-fronted body with recessed windscreen, not unlike that of Park Royal bodies for underfloor-engines chassis though the multi-windowed side is reminiscent of older American practice. It is thought to have been built by Longwell Green (a plate in the cab bears the number 14663) and the vehicle was a one-off export via H. Torrendell in 1955, but the body sides may have been replaced later. The retention of a near facsimile of the grille outline, complete with ACLO badge, is noteworthy especially as the front of this vehicle appears to have been tidied up more recently than the rest of the body. The front bumper appears to be of the type made by Pyrene, usually chromium-plated originally, often fitted to export British buses. It now has a Brazilian-made Perkins engine and gearbox, Mike reporting that it makes a frightful din within.

The Regal IV, 9831E385, was taken up with similar enthusiasm by South American operators. This example, built for C.U.T.C.S.A. in 1954, has Crossley bodywork of the style favoured for Park Royal and Crossley export single-deckers in the 'fifties and seen in right-hand form on the vehicles of Christchurch, New Zealand pictured on an earlier page. It had collected some minor blemishes but was remarkably free from damage or modification from original form, save replacement of the gearbox by a Leyland Pneumocyclic unit, when seen in October 1991. It was used by a meat processing factory near San José when seen but the livery indicated earlier ownership by Castro.

Sales of ACLO buses to Uruguayan operators continued into the Regal VI period. Number 85 of the COTSUR fleet heels slightly as it rounds a curve in Montevideo. Four identical buses were seen in COTSUR's blue, yellow and white livery. The styling of the side windows shows evidence of influence from the General Motors 'New Look' design on the Parco Polo bodywork, from Caxias de Sul Brazil.

Some operators' vehicles have received modifications over the years. The Mercedes-Benz three-pointed star, a utilitarian small front grille and increased clearance under the wheel arches of this Reliance of Empresa Omnibus San Antonio's number 6 are clues to the installation of a front-mounted Mercedes-Benz engine and gearbox, yet the ACLO badge remains in place. It was imported to Uruguay complete and the body seems likely to be by Verhaul. The operator's only other vehicle was a Mercedes-Benz.

In December 1962, AEC invited the technical press to Southall to view one of 150 ACLO Regal VI models with bodywork by Verheul, at that date described as "AEC's associate coachwork concern in Holland", for two newly-formed co-operative undertakings in Montevideo. Of these, 100 were for C.O.E.T.C., which had links with the existing C.U.T.C.S.A., and 50 for U.C.O.T., similarly related to A.M.D.E.T. and further orders were expected to follow. They were on U2LA chassis with AH690 engines and Monocontrol transmission and were of 11-metre length, the bodywork seating 40 passengers and with standing room for 60. An example of the type, probably that used for the press demonstration, is seen outside the AEC Service Department building at Southall. It was reported that orders for nearly 700 bus chassis had been received from South America – including over 500 by the Argentine government for service in Buenos Aires – in "the past year".

It virtually goes without saying that such comparative youngsters among Uruguayan AEC buses should still be in service, but this Mike Fenton photograph of September last shows U2LA663 in virtually unchanged condition, save for a sun visor added over the windscreen. The C.O.E.T.C. livery, ACLO and Verheul emblems and wheel nut guard ring, all remain and the overall condition of number 54, apart from deterioration of paintwork towards the rear of the roof, would do credit to a much newer vehicle. The C.O.E.T.C. fleet of about 100 buses is still about 90% of this type – livery is light grey, red and white.

Not all the Verheul-bodied Regal VI buses carry their years quite as well, and U.C.O.T. number 49 bears the scars of some traffic encounters. More significantly, a Mercedes-Benz badge and a grille in the rearmost side panel are clues to a re-engining exercise – six vehicles of about 50 of the type still in service (roughly half the fleet) had rear-mounted M-B 145 engines and gearboxes.

Uruguay's stock of old AEC vehicles is not confined to buses. Brian Goulding found these examples of Mandator Mark III models around the docks area in Montevideo during a visit in 1984, but it is probable that they or other vehicles like them (for many were seen on that occasion), are still in use. The cab style is clearly related to the standard AEC-design unit as built in Britain but a little more rounded in American style, especially at the rear, and the outward swivelling quarter lights are noteworthy, though the windscreens appear to be fixed.

More modern and still very smartly-kept at that date, was this Mandator of the tilt-cab type, with Colonia licence plate, very much like contemporary home-market production apart from the left-hand steering, ACLO badge and the divided windscreen which seems to have been more common on export examples. It was in the fleet of Carlos Patron, faithful to AEC for many years and who had several Mark III and Mark V models on quite long-distance routes into Argentina.
(B. Goulding)

More modern ACLO vehicles operated by C.U.T.C.S.A., one of the main bus co-operatives in Montevideo include these two examples. On the left is number 841, a Ranger, photographed by Brian Goulding during his visit – at the time C.U.T.C.S.A. had 44 Rangers.

Some 20 left-hand drive Ranger chassis were sold to C.U.T.C.S.A. in the early 'eighties, having been part of a batch of 30 thought to have been the last AEC chassis to leave Southall after its closure, apparently being part of a cancelled order from the middle east. They stood in AEC's former depot in Nottingham for nearly two years before sale, ten going to Cyprus (where they were rebuilt to right-hand for Lefkaritis Bros) but those for Uruguay were dismantled and exported CKD by a subsidiary of Marshall Bros Transport at Bulwell, themselves old AEC customers. They were bodied in C.U.T.C.S.A.'s own workshops, some with three doors, as shown, and some with two, operating on express services around Montevideo. This one was photographed by Mike Fenton. He reports that they are not well liked and difficulty in getting spares resulted in some being fitted with Mercedes-Benz engines in place of the original units.

15 – Argentina

Despite the problems of a decade ago, ACLO vehicles can still be found in Argentina – in fact that country still has many examples of British influence, an example being seen in the address quoted on the side of this furniture van. It was photographed by Mike Fenton during a visit in September 1991. Based on a Regal VI chassis, what appears to be the original coach body has been repanelled for the vehicle's current role. In the 'sixties, ACLO buses and coaches were still being supplied to Argentina at a rate of hundreds per year.

The ACLO trade mark, which replaced the AEC mark on vehicles built for South America, Spain and, at least in theory, Germany, was introduced when AEG, the big German electric concern, objected to the use of AEC in those markets, even though its only competitive products were battery electric vehicles. The NS demonstrator shown above is thought to have been the first to carry the ACLO name. The precise significance, if any, of the letters was not explained but something like 'Associated Company, Lorry Omnibus' or maybe even 'London Omnibuses' seems likely, though the 'C' **could** relate to 'camiones', the Spanish for lorries. It remained in use to the end of production.

Sales of AEC-built buses to South America were firmly established in the mid-'twenties. A notable venture was the dispatch of this NS-type demonstrator with ACLO radiator emblem to Buenos Aires, Argentina, in January 1925. It was of covered-top pattern, something which had yet to be seen in service in London, thanks to the cautious attitude of the Metropolitan Police, though almost identical vehicles were eventually permitted to enter service there, at first experimentally, from the autumn of that year. This was only one of several overseas ventures by AEC double-deck demonstrators in the 'twenties, some of them to unlikely-seeming cities. Buenos Aires did not favour the double-decker, but 40 chassis of the same 409 model, though with pneumatic tyres, were supplied for use as single-deckers to Anglo-Argentine Tramways Co, operating in Buenos Aires, later in 1925, the low-frame chassis proving attractive. Short Bros built the body for the demonstrator.   (AEC)

16 – Peru

The Verheul-bodied ACLO Regal VI attracted interest from other areas in South America. A front-engined Regal had been demonstrated in Lima, Peru, in 1931 and although not as big a market for ACLO vehicles as Argentina, Brazil or Uruguay, that country did place some orders in later years, an agency being held by Peruvian Autos Ltda. The body design of this Regal VI operated by Surco in Lima is almost identical to those supplied for service in Montevideo. (AEC)

This photograph was used on the front cover of AEC Gazette for March-April 1963, and shows one of 60 then new Reliance buses for National Transit System and Princes Town Special Bus Services, holders of the sole concessions for bus operation in North Trinidad and South Trinidad respectively, under a reorganisation of transport on the island. It is seen outside White Hall, the office of the Prime Minister of Trinidad and Tobago, in Port of Spain. The vehicle shown was one of 45 for National Transit with bodywork ordered from the Duple concern but built by Burlingham, which had then recently become part of the Duple group and whose Blackpool factory later became Duple's main base when it moved from Hendon in north west London. Some of these vehicles can still be found in scrapyards at the southern end of the island. (AEC)

17 – West Indies

Although nominally a Scammell, this six-wheel recovery vehicle operated by the Trinidad & Tobago Fire service and seen by Brian Goulding in February 1992 at the main fire station in Port of Spain, Trinidad, is virtually a 'pure' AEC '690-type' Dumptruk, albeit probably assembled at Watford. The engine was an L12 – the uprated AV760 – and the running units were of AEC design; the gearchange plate in the cab bore the AEC-Southall triangle.

The odd AEC goods model is still to be seen in the West Indies. This Mammoth Major (TG6RB685) is a former RAF 3000-gal refuelling tanker and was imported as such before being converted locally for haulage work. It was seen at a yard in Bridgetown, Barbados – several other Mammoth Majors and a Marathon were observed on haulage work in Barbados during the same trip. (B. Goulding)

18 – Canada

Although North America was always a difficult area for British commercial vehicle exports, AEC obtained a modest though quite prestigious foothold in Canada with the Ranger normal-control passenger model in the early 'thirties. The British Columbia Electric Railway Co was an early customer, this example of a left-hand drive model dating from about 1931. (AEC)

A little later, the emphasis shifted to coach versions of the Ranger and Gray Coach Lines Ltd of Toronto used this 1932 Ranger and another like it on its route to Buffalo. The bodywork, with distinct echoes of American railway observation car practice in its rear-end styling, was by Canadian Car & Foundry Co of Montreal, later a vehicle builder, using AEC engines in post-war years. The chassis had a petrol engine, fluid flywheel, preselective gearbox, and Lockheed hydraulic brakes. Interestingly, Gray Coach Lines was purchased by Stagecoach Holdings Ltd in 1990 and is thus now part of that familiar British-owned bus-operating group. (AEC)

By a nice coincidence, a firm called Gray Line, thought to be a subsidiary of the Toronto concern, was operating ex-London Transport RT3159, nominally dating from 1950, one of six licensed for sightseeing duty in Victoria, British Columbia, in March 1980. London, or London-style, double-deckers are to be found as a tourist attraction in various places in North America. Perhaps the most remarkable is in the town of Davis, near Sacramento, California, where the Unitrans fleet of 33 buses regularly serving a branch of the University of California and the local community includes six ex-London RT buses and an RTL, dating from 1948-54. We are obliged to Michael Dryhurst, nowadays a California resident, for the information – latest news is that two of the RTs have Cummins B-series engines and Allison automatic gearboxes, two have Leyland 0.600 engines, but it is planned to keep one vehicle, RT742, with original engine and transmission..
(Brian Goulding)

Acknowledgements

It is never possible to be comprehensive in thanking all those who have helped in the compilation of a book of this kind. Some did so quite unknowingly, often many years ago, by contributing to the pool of knowledge of the authors, both of whom are enthusiasts of the AEC marque since their youth. Others have given more specific help by supplying information or photographs. Sadly there simply isn't space to include all, for the reaction to both general invitations and more specific enquiries has been almost overwhelming, making the task of editing fascinating but yet often difficult in deciding what to use from so much material.

The origin of the photograph is conveyed wherever possible in the captions. We are fortunate in that AEC had, and made good use of, a skilled photographic department, and many examples of its work are reproduced by courtesy of the British Commercial Vehicle Museum and from the authors' and other collections. Similar remarks apply to other official sources, notably bodybuilders' official views.

Prominent among individuals who have helped in supplying material or information for this book are the following:–

W. S. N. (Bill) Barlow, Gordon Baron, Tony Blackman, John Burton, Malcolm Castle, Dick Cuff, Peter J. Davies, R. C. (Bob) Davis, Mike Dryhurst, Graham Edge, Mike Fenton, Flt. Lt. Keith Hunter, Carl Ireland, Michael McGeeham, Roy Marshall, J. Muncie, D. A. (Tony) Peart, Harry Pick, Leo Pratt, Paul Richman, Clive Screaton, John Shearman, Nick Shipsey, W. J. (Bill) Taylor, Ken Topping, Norman Tuckwell, Gerald Truran, Barry Weatherhead and David Whittaker.

From abroad, mention must be made of the following:–

Australia – Chris Goodsall, Tony Petch. New Zealand – David Jones and the Omnibus Society (Inc) of NZ, Brian Bickmore. South Africa – Ken Froud, Bill Bolton, Derek Bolton.

Many of these are united by membership of the AEC Society, without which the breadth of content in this volume, especially of vehicles still in existence in so many parts of the world, would have been impossible.

What can be regarded as 'stop press' pictures which arrived just before going to press include two taken by Brian Goulding in June 1992. On the left is one of the two Regent III buses now preserved in Lisbon by Carris, seen outside the Miraflores depot. Number 486 originally entered service as a single-decker with Saunders body in 1950, though because of the bodybuilding delays of those days its chassis, 9631E472, is about two years older still, though rebodied locally in later years to a very Weymann-like style.

Passing through Santander in Spain on the same trip, Brian saw the vehicle shown above still in service with Autocars J. Arroyo, and looking and sounding very good. It is said to date from 1962 and was described as a Barreiros-engined ACLO chassis but Brian thinks it is an early Barreiros-AEC. Barreiros-AEC S.A. was formed in 1961 as a joint venture to build chassis based on the Reliance design in Madrid, though contemporary AEC publicity indicated that the first vehicle was not completed until 1963, with an initial contract of 110. Barreiros was already well established as a commercial vehicle manufacturer.

The latest addition to Clive Screaton's Grand European Touring Company fleet based in Warrington is this 1934 Regal, FV 45448, newly refurbished. It entered service with William Salisbury Ltd of Blackpool, and originally had a Beadle rear-entrance coach body. The firm was taken over by W. C. Standerwick Ltd, Ribble's coaching subsidiary, also based in Blackpool, operating in that fleet until impressed for RAF service in 1941. When returned to Ribble in 1946 it was placed in service as an instruction bus and continued thus until sold to the dealer North, of Leeds, in 1957. It was doubtless in this period that it acquired a 7.7-litre oil engine and a Leyland coach body from one of Ribble's batch of Leyland Tiger TS6 coaches of 1933, most of which had been used by the War Department, from 1940, none with this type of body returning to service with Ribble after the war. In later years it was acquired for preservation and for some time ran in the livery of the former Gower Vanguard concern of Swansea. (Clive Screaton)